JACK KEROUAC

Tracing the Theme of Epiphany

First Edition

By Evert Villarreal

The University of Texas—Rio Grande Valley

cognella® | ACADEMIC PUBLISHING

Bassim Hamadeh, CEO and Publisher
John Remington, Senior Field Acquisitions Editor
Gem Rabanera, Project Editor
Casey Hands, Associate Production Editor
Emely Villavicencio, Senior Graphic Designer
Trey Soto, Licensing Coordinator
Natalie Piccotti, Director of Marketing
Kassie Graves, Vice President of Editorial
Jamie Giganti, Director of Academic Publishing

Copyright © 2019 by Cognella, Inc. All rights reserved. No part of this publication may be reprinted, reproduced, transmitted, or utilized in any form or by any electronic, mechanical, or other means, now known or hereafter invented, including photocopying, microfilming, and recording, or in any information retrieval system without the written permission of Cognella, Inc. For inquiries regarding permissions, translations, foreign rights, audio rights, and any other forms of reproduction, please contact the Cognella Licensing Department at rights@cognella.com.

Trademark Notice: Product or corporate names may be trademarks or registered trademarks, and are used only for identification and explanation without intent to infringe.

Cover image: Copyright © 2009 iStockphoto LP/JTBurrell.

Printed in the United States of America.

ISBN: 978-1-5165-3396-1 (pbk) / 978-1-5165-3397-8 (br)

Table of Contents

This book is dedicated with profound and endless love and affection to ISABEL, my beautiful, brilliant, and wonderful wife!
Once again, she has served as my muse!
She is the yellow in my sunshine!

ALSO, for MATTHEW, THOMAS, and LUKE—our wonderful sons!
The four members of my family are truly the inspiration
for everything I do in life.

ALSO, with profound love and admiration to my parents,
SABAS and BETTY VILLARREAL, who have taught me the value of hard work and have given me the life-long gift of optimism. They have always insisted that my life reflect a continuous journey to excellence, with no excuses.

ADDITIONALLY, this book is dedicated to my brother,
EDGAR VILLARREAL, who has always supported my professional career and is always there to lend a hand.

FINALLY, to ALL MY STUDENTS, who have taught me so much over the last twenty-three years of college teaching.

Introduction

J ack Kerouac's books deserve attention because each work reveals the mind of a very deep thinker who is sincerely trying to understand the complex journey of life. According to Allen Ginsberg, Jack Kerouac's life and works reveal a strong interest in the Buddha's idea of *dukkha* or the idea of transitoriness, which can be understood—to some extent—as suffering or pain (physical, emotional, and mental). The idea of *dukkha* also encompasses the idea of the awareness of impermanence or change in anything that is not permanent, including happiness and great success. A third idea of *dukkha* focuses on conditioned states; in other words, awareness of the understanding that we are dependent on others and an awareness that we are continuously affected by others or something else: all phenomena are conditioned. Kerouac biographer Tom Clark believes that Kerouac had what Aristotle called *"nous"*—an apperceptive intelligence—where a person makes sense of an idea by assimilating it to the body of ideas he or she already possesses.

Jack Kerouac's influence on American culture is profound—the hippies of the 1960s counter-culture idolized him, although he repudiated them. His influence on American writers is significant, although his place in the literary canon is still uncertain.

His works, written over a twenty-year period from 1946 to 1967 reveal a constant and dynamic search for epiphany, and this is what this book examines.

Acknowledgments

For help and generosity with information, materials, feedback as well as professional support and encouragement of one sort or another, I am grateful to Dr. Lee T. Hamilton, Dr. Rebekah Hamilton, Dr. James Haule, Dr. Donald Fritz, Dr. Adelle Mery, Dr. Rob Johnson, Dr. Michael Faubion, Dr. Raymond Welch, Dr. Valerie Reimers, Mr. Bud Frankenberger, Dr. William Bedford Clark, Dr. Clinton Machann, Dr. Valerie Balester, Dr. Dennis Berthold, Dr. Howard Marchitello, Dr. Marco Portales and Dr. Terence Hoagwood. I also wish to thank Mr. Tim Benavides and Mrs. Maria Benavides for all they do!

Also, for friendship and support of one kind or another, I am indebted to Dr. Michael Hannaman, M.D., Mr. Wade Kokernot, and Mr. Jaime Cantu. Additionally, for friendship and support I wish to thank Dr. Allan Goren, Dr. Amy Becker-Chambless, Dr. Robert Moreira, Dr. Shawn Thomson, Dr. Amy Cummins, Dr. David Anshen, Dr. Gary Schneider, Dr. David Bowles, Dr. Douglas LaPrade, Dr. Caroline Miles, Dr. Linda Belau, Dr. Ed Cameron, and Dr. Michael Reed—all valued colleagues at The University of Texas Rio Grande Valley.

Chronology of Jack Kerouac's Life 1922-1969

1922 Born Jean-Louis Lebris de Kerouac in Lowell, Massachusetts on March 12; third child of Gabrielle and Leo Kerouac, French-Canadian immigrants to New England.

1926 Kerouac's older brother Gerard dies of rheumatic fever at the age of nine. Kerouac becomes very introverted after the death of his older brother. He also believes that his brother followed him throughout life serving as a guardian angel.

1928 On May 17 Jack experienced his first Sacrament of Confession at the age of six. During his stay at a rosary (to practice penance), Jack imagined that he could hear God who told him he had a good soul but he would have to suffer in his life and would die a painful and horror-filled life, but would receive salvation in the end.

1928 Learns to speak English.

1939 Graduates from Lowell High School.

1939 Attends Horace Mann Preparatory School, New York City. Offered football scholarships from Boston University, Notre Dame University, and Columbia.

1940 Attends Columbia College, NY on a football scholarship. Played for iconic coach Luigi "Lou Little" Piccolo, who coached at Columbia from 1930-1956.

1941 Enrolls in courses with Professor Mark Van Doren at Columbia.

1941 Because of his truancy in school and tense relationship with Coach Piccolo, he loses football scholarship and leaves Columbia.

1942 Sails to Greenland as merchant marine on S. S. *Dorchester*. Writes his first novel, *The Sea is My Brother*, which was published almost seventy years later in 2011.

1943 Enlists in U.S. Navy, discharged after only eight days of active duty on psychiatric grounds. Sails to Liverpool as merchant seaman on S.S. *George Weems*.

1944 Meets Edie Parker who introduces him to Allen Ginsberg, William S. Burroughs, Lucien Carr, and Herbert Huncke. Jailed as accessory and material witness in David Kammerer murder case (who was killed by Lucien Carr). Marries Edie Parker, a student at Barnard.

1945 Meets Neal Cassady in New York.

1946 Marriage with Edie Parker annulled. Collaborates with William Burroughs on an unpublished novel, *And the Hippos Were Boiled in Their Tanks*, an account of the events surrounding the Kammerer murder. Leo Kerouac (Jack's father) dies of cancer of the stomach at the age of 56.

1946 From 1946 to 1949, he writes over 1,200 pages of the first draft of *The Town and the City*. The book was heavily edited by Robert Giroux at Harcourt Brace, who cut over 400 pages.

1947 From 1947 to 1948, he travels to Denver, California, and back to New York, often with Neal Cassady.

1948 Meets John Clellon Holmes. Kerouac coins the term "Beat Generation", which he explains as being "sympathetic."

1948 Begins working on earliest version of *On the Road.*

1949 Travels with Cassady to Louisiana and San Francisco. Moves briefly to Colorado with mother (*Memere*). Visits San Francisco. Returns with Cassady to New York.

1950 *The Town and The City* published. Many positive reviews of the first novel. Travels to Denver, then with Cassady to Mexico. Marries Joan Haverty in New York.

1951 Reads manuscripts of William Burroughs's *Junkie* and John Clellon Holmes's *Go* in February/March. Writes *On The Road*, the third version, on one single 120-foot roll of paper in three weeks during April and May (6,500 words a day for 20 days). Separates from Joan Haverty. Discovers compositional method of "sketching" or "spontaneous prose" and begins to rewrite *On the Road* and the experimental book *Visions of Cody*; continues work of the latter novel into 1952 at Neal Cassady's home in San Francisco. Kerouac is hospitalized with thrombophlebitis as a result of heavy Benzedrine use. Travels to California.

1952 Writes *Dr. Sax* in Burroughs's apartment in Mexico City. Travels to North Carolina to visit sister Caroline in Rocky Mount, back to California where he works as a student brakeman and writes "The Railroad Earth" in California and Mexico before returning to New York. Daughter Jan Kerouac born in Albany, New York.

1953 Writes *Maggie Cassidy* while in New York. Travels to California; works on railroad; takes job on S.S. *William Carruth*; leaves *Carruth* in New Orleans. Writes *The Subterraneans* (in only three days) in New York. Writes "The Essentials of Spontaneous Prose" in which he articulates many of his writing principles.

1954 Visits Neal Cassady in San Jose. Studies Buddhism in New York and California. Writes *San Francisco Blues* in San Francisco; *Some of the Dharma* in New York and North Carolina. Writes *Book of Dreams*.

1955 Travels to Mexico City where he writes *Mexico City Blues* and begins *Tristessa*. Meets Gary Snyder and attends "Six Poets at the Six Gallery" reading in San Francisco on Oct. 13 where Ginsberg first reads "Howl." Writes a biography of Siddhartha Gautama titled *Wake Up: A Life of the Buddha* published in 2008.

1956 Writes *Visions of Gerard* in North Carolina. Travels to California; stays in Marin County. Writes *The Scripture of the Golden Eternity* and *Old Angel Midnight*. Works as fire lookout (for sixty-three days, sixty days in complete isolation) in Mt. Baker National Forest, Washington, where he writes the journals that would become Book One of *Desolation Angels*. Finishes *Tristessa* in Mexico City where he prepares Book One of *Desolation Angels*. Returns to New York. Ginsberg's *Howl and Other Poems* published by City Lights in San Francisco.

1957 Travels to Tangier, Morocco where he types and edits Burroughs's *Naked Lunch* with Ginsberg, then on to Paris and London. After returning to New York where he meets and lives with Joyce Johnson. Visits Mexico City briefly; moves to Orlando, Florida with his mother. Travels to New York. During this time *On the Road* is published and Kerouac gives readings at the Village Vanguard. Writes *The Dharma Bums* in Orlando. Gilbert Millstein's now famous review of *On the Road* appeared in *The New York Times*, proclaiming Kerouac the voice of a new generation. Kerouac soon came to be known as "the king of the Beat Generation."

1958 Buys home in Northport, Long Island. *The Subterraneans* and *The Dharma Bums* are published. Neal Cassady sentenced to five years in San Quentin for possession of marijuana. Begins writing sketches for *Lonesome Traveler*.

1959 Narrates film *Pull My Daisy* in New York which is based on his play, *The Beat Generation*. Begins writing column for *Escapade*. *Dr. Sax*, *Mexico City Blues*, and *Maggie Cassidy* published. Travels to Los Angeles for *Steve Allen Show* appearance.

1959 Studio albums with Steve Allen titled *Poetry for the Beat Generation and Blues and Haikus* (with Al Cohn and Zoot Sims).

1960 Travels to California, stays at Bixby Canyon (Big Sur); suffers alcohol withdrawal and nervous breakdown. Returns to New York. *Tristessa* and *Lonesome Traveler* published.

1960 Studio album: *Readings by Jack Kerouac on the Beat Generation*

1961 *Book of Dreams* published. Moves to Orlando with mother. Travels to Mexico City, where he writes Book Two ("Passing Through") of *Desolation Angels*. Returns to Florida, where he writes *Big Sur*.

1962 Moves back to Northport with mother. *Big Sur* published.

1963 *Visions of Gerard* published.

1964 Moves with mother to St. Petersburg, Florida. Sister Caroline dies. Meets Ken Kesey in New York with the Merry Pranksters. Neal Cassady is the driver. It is the first time Kerouac and Cassady have seen each other in years.

1965 Travels to France. Writes *Satori in Paris* and *Pic* in Florida. *Desolation Angels* published.

1966 *Satori in Paris* published. Moves to Hyannis, Massachusetts, with mother who suffers a paralyzing stroke. Marries Stella Sampas, sister of childhood friend Sebastian Sampas.

1967 Moves to Lowell with mother and wife. Writes *Vanity of Duluoz*.

1968 Neal Cassady dies in Mexico. *Vanity of Duluoz* published. Travels to Europe with friends. Appears on *Firing Line* hosted by William F. Buckley, which would be his last television appearance before his death. Moves with mother and wife to St. Petersburg, Florida. Neal Cassady dies in Mexico.

1969 Dies in St. Petersburg, Oct. 20, of abdominal hemorrhage due to complications associated with alcohol abuse. He was only 47 years old.

1971 *Pic* published.

1973 *Visions of Cody* published. Jack Kerouac's mother dies.

1977 *Heaven and Other Poems* published.

1992 *Poems All Sizes* published.

1993 *Old Angel Midnight* and *Good Blonde & Others* published.

1995 *Book of Blues* and *Selected Letters: 1940-1956* published.

1996 Jan Kerouac (Kerouac's daughter) dies at the age of 44.

1997 *On The Road: 40th Anniversary Edition* and *Some of the Dharma* published. Allen Ginsberg dies.

2001 Jim Irsay, owner of the Indianapolis Colts, buys the original 120-foot scroll of *On the Road*. He paid $2.4 million dollars, making *On the Road* the most expensive literary manuscript ever sold.

2007 Honored posthumously with a degree of Doctor of Letters from his hometown University of Massachusetts Lowell.

Books by Jack Kerouac

The Town and the City, 1950
On the Road, 1957
The Subterraneans, 1958
The Dharma Bums, 1958
Dr. Sax, 1959
Maggie Cassidy, 1959
Mexico City Blues: 242 Choruses, 1959
Book of Dreams, 1960
Tristessa, 1960
Visions of Cody, 1960
The Scripture of the Golden Eternity, 1960
Lonesome Traveler, 1960
Pull My Daisy, 1961
Big Sur, 1962
Visions of Gerard, 1963
Desolation Angels, 1965
Satori in Paris, 1966
Vanity of Duluoz, 1968
Pic, 1971
Scattered Poems, 1971
Old Angel Midnight, 1973
Trip Trap: Haiku on the Road (with Albert Saijo & Lew Welch), 1973
Heaven and Other Poems, 1977

San Francisco Blues, 1991
Poems All Sizes, 1992
Good Blonde and Others, 1993
Book of Blues, 1995
Some of the Dharma, 1997
Atop an Underwood: Early Stories and Other Writings, 1999
Orpheus Emerged, 2000
Book of Dreams (Enlarged edition), 2001
Book of Haikus, 2003
Wake Up: A Life of the Buddha, 2008
And the Hippos Were Boiled in Their Tanks, 2010
The Sea Is My Brother, 2012

Chapter 1

The Historical, Cultural, and Literary Context that Gave Rise to the Beat Generation

Twentieth century literature has grown and expanded in its experimentalism, keeping pace with the furious technological and geographical expansion of the country. As a carryover from the wide-ranging literature of the nineteenth century, the twentieth century has also seen many writers and poets who have expressed their disapproval of society's changes, others have voiced their approval, and still others have focused on making ahistorical comments on the human species and the human condition. If we briefly examine literature in the twentieth century, we will see that many writers during different periods have expressed a strong sense of loss (both psychological and spiritual) and the movement in the 1940s, 1950s, and 1960s—known as the Beat Generation—is no exception. The literary coalition formed by the members of the Beat Generation, whose tenets were expressed principally by Jack Kerouac, Allen Ginsberg, Gregory Corso, William Burroughs, and many others, focused not only on directly criticizing conservative society, but more importantly, on finding answers to make some sense of the world in which they lived.

This sense of loss can be seen directly in how these writers, and many others that followed, experimented tremendously with subject matter and technique. This experimentalism violated many, if not all, pre-established rules of style used in literature as writers and poets searched to find new artistic techniques that they believed were more authentic and liberating. This sense of loss can also be seen in the increasing overall secularism of our society, and as a result, in three central themes that have emerged in twentieth century literature: a sense of decay in religion and religious institutions, a sense that there is death in life, and a growing sense that there is sterility and meaninglessness in the idea and concept of love. As a result, many writers have attempted to make meaning out of this sense of loss.

1

At the start of the twentieth century, American literature began to change dramatically as writers began to express a growing feeling of angst. The writers' and poets' feelings of disorientation, to a great extent, were caused by the growth and expansion of technology and industry that came as a result of the Industrial Revolution. At the end of the nineteenth century, for the first time in American history "the small farming community was replaced, as America saw a large migration into the urban areas of its large cities. The creation of the automobile gave individual Americans an acquired mobility unimaginable to previous generations" (Baym, 940). Experimentalism with electricity and its far-reaching influences as well as the use of radio and the telephone also grew. These helped give rise to the industrial age of America, which gave rise to assembly lines and the mass production of goods. Social needs and impersonal jobs working in large factories where the individual could easily be replaced by another worker in line for a minimum wage job, helped lead to the decline of the individual's sense of identity. Many writers and poets believed that the Industrial Revolution contributed to the decline of our nation, "criticizing the commercialism and manipulativeness of our culture" (Baym, 940). As a result, commercialism, urbanization, and industrialization were becoming inherent parts of the American way of life and were slowly altering and changing the values of our society. All of these forces would later culminate with America's involvement in World War I and World War II.

The growth of modern science also led to several intellectual developments that refuted many of the nineteenth century-accepted explanations as to how the universe worked, and instead revealed the uncertainty of our knowledge of how the universe really operates. "For many literary intellectuals, especially the more conservative, the chief problem raised by expansion of scientific authority was the corresponding loss of authority for traditional, humanistic explanations of the real world and human life" (Baym, 941). Along with many others, three key figures of monumental importance that challenged the established beliefs of how the universe operates were Charles Darwin, Sigmund Freud, and Albert Einstein.

The publication of *On the Origin of Species* in 1859 by the British naturalist Charles Darwin promoted and explained the theory he had developed. The theory of evolution based on natural selection explained how only the fittest of animals and different species survived over time, and how all species must adapt to their surroundings or die, human beings being no exception.

Darwin speculated that the race of humans might have developed from a lower life form and, through the course of evolution, evolved into *Homo sapiens*. His book and theories indirectly challenged and refuted the "Myth of Creation" and also made less necessary the idea of the existence of God, or a supreme being. No longer was mankind seen as a species that had been divinely placed on earth by God; instead, many people began to believe the idea that *Homo sapiens* were here simply because we had evolved. Darwin's theories stripped away much of the mystery, magic, and respect that mankind had placed in God for thousands of years, and, although only a theory, its effects altered the views that mankind had about itself and made us question our own genetic origins.

The Austrian Sigmund Freud was another key figure of monumental importance who challenged the established beliefs of how the universe operates. He was the founder of psychoanalysis, and the horrors of World War I as well as the precarious nature of peace in the post-war years led him to meditate on the nature of civilization. Freud was primarily interested in the conflicts between individuals and their society, and reflection led him to trace the origins of civilized life back to its sources in the human psyche (Smith, 339). His theories on the complexity of identity formation also added to the intellectual developments taking place at the beginning of the twentieth century. Generally, Freud stated that all human thought, including dreams, was a crucial part of every person's sense of identity. Freud stated that the person that we really want to be, a self-indulgent animal, must be repressed. In order to fit into society, mankind's base, animalistic urges must be repressed, and the rapaciously selfish individuals that we really want to be must be forced to conform to the rules society infringes upon us. Freud also further undermined established religious beliefs:

> Freud defined religion as an illusion inspired by an infantile belief in the omnipotence of thought, i.e., a universal neurosis, and kind of narcotic that hampers the free exercise of intelligence, something that man will have to give up. (Smith, 340)

Freud concluded that, unfortunately, for mankind's view of civilization to survive, individuals must give up their personal wants and conform to what is best for the group. In toto, his work on psychoanalysis opened up a universe that made individuals more aware of the complexity of what goes in the making and production of our identities and what goes into the making of the mental structures of awareness described as the unconscious, preconscious, and conscious mind.

Finally, Albert Einstein and his theories of relativity also helped to profoundly revolutionize modern thought:

> Twentieth century human beings were well aware that a world composed of subatomic particles, a world in which matter and energy, space and time, interpenetrate, a world in which scientific laws like "relativity" and "uncertainty" (Werner Heisenberg), is a world in which nothing is as it appears to be to the human senses. What the early twentieth century witnessed was what Nietzsche had prophesied: a radical questioning of the Greco-Roman and Judeo-Christian roots of our culture. Reason and authority, humanism and faith, the pillars of these cultures, were undermined as never before. (Smith, 332)

Einstein's theory of relativity simply stated that, although we may not realize it, there are many particular arrangements working together that make life possible and, if any of those elements is ever missing or altered, all forms of life on Earth might easily disappear.

As a result of these, and many other intellectual developments, artists from around the world reacted fervently. The artistic movement known as Modernism responded to this sense of social breakdown; the Dada movement was one of its many sub-movements. This European artistic movement allowed artists to do whatever they wanted with their art, even if all traditional rules were broken. Artists felt that art should reflect "the randomness and pessimism that is bred by the recognition of man's inability to control his life" (Smith, 356). Artists painted, wrote, and composed for themselves believing it was the observer's responsibility to find or make some sense of the meaning of their work as they articulated their own particular worldview.

Art, therefore, became a way of "experiencing the world" and gave individual artists an outlet for expressing their own worldview. This consignment of and confidence in the artistic expression of art became unique, special, and strong. Many writers and artists found that art served as a vehicle for articulating criticisms of the society and world in which they lived. And, more importantly, art also allowed individual artists to find their own meaning and make some *sense* of the world around them. What resulted was a modernist movement like no other before. Art saw major shifts from the traditional canonized styles with artists experimenting widely with different genres such as painting, sculpture, architecture, music, dance, photography, and film.

In summary, American society in the early part of the last century was not only being bombarded by industrial expansion and growth, but was also inescapably having to examine and question the intellectual developments that were shaking the foundations that made up the moral fiber of our society, and, more importantly, the very nature of existence.

In addition to all of these social, cultural shifts, and artistic shifts, US involvement in World War I was an event that was to change America forever. It was also an event that declared the United States as a world power: "More narrowly but more immediately, it involved American artists and thinkers with the brutal actualities of large-scale modern war, so different from imaginary heroism" (Baym, 939). American artists and thinkers were affected tremendously by the massive destruction and death that spread over the European landscape, and were horrified by mankind's struggle for power and control at any cost. This war played a major role in beginning the breakdown of confidence in the civilization known as mankind. The war made a damning statement about us and our priorities, ultimately placing little value on human life, either as individuals or *en masse*. Not only was Europe involved in this first great war, but the entire world saw its many countries divided and fighting, either to invade other countries or defending themselves from invasion. It was this large-scale involvement that first led to feelings of hopelessness in humankind and resulted in the knowledge and fear that worldwide destruction was indeed possible. Writers, poets, and artists soon began to write and paint as a way to express their growing displeasure with what mankind was doing to itself; the war was seen as a sign of the social breakdown that was festering and spreading.

World War I and America's participation in it marked a turning point that established the country as a world power. Unfortunately, the staggering losses of life, land, and property had been enormous in Europe, and it became difficult for anyone to say what had been gained after the protracted conflict. More importantly, however, the war led to an "increased feeling of social breakdown, and of individual powerlessness" (Baym, 939) and produced "resulting feelings of fear and disorientation" (Baym, 939). World War I also created growing feelings of angst in the lives of writers and artists, both in Europe and in America.

A great deal of the serious literature "written between 1914 and 1945 attempted to convey a vision of social decay through appropriate techniques, or offered radical critiques of American society on behalf of working people, or tried to develop a conservative literature that could counter social breakdown" (Baym, 944). To simplify the twentieth century literary movement, we can say that writers before World War I had some degree of faith in both society and art, writers between 1914 and 1945 had faith in art alone, and writers after 1945 had lost faith in both society and art, and were left to find faith in their own individuality and existence.

World War II almost seemed like a continuation of World War I; however, in contrast to World War I, civilians suffered more casualties than did the military. The systematic extermination of populations by the Germans and the intensive bombing of cities by both sides explain the large losses. The introduction of the atomic bomb at the very end of the war dramatically illustrated what would occur in the event of a third world war. This apprehension was only exacerbated by the introduction of an arms race in nuclear weapons, which began with the Soviet development of its own atomic bomb in 1946 (Smith, 432).

In addition, the atrocities committed by Joseph Stalin, Mao Zedong, and Adolf Hitler showed horrendous barbarity never seen before in world history.

This background information leads us to the focus of this book: the emergence of the Beat Generation and, more specifically, the search for epiphany in the writings of Jack Kerouac. The Beat Generation took root in the aftermath of World War II, after the genocide of the Jews instigated by Adolf Hitler, known as "The Final Solution," and after the massive destruction of Hiroshima and Nagasaki with atomic bombs in August of 1945.

It was this fear of annihilation that set the backdrop for the emergence of the Beats. "The postwar era was a time of extraordinary insecurity, of profound powerlessness as far as individual effort was concerned, when personal responsibility was being abdicated in favor of corporate largeness, when the catchwords were coordination and adjustment . . ." (Tytell, 5). The sense of hope that had for so long been visible in the "American Dream" had been destroyed, and the youth of the time felt a great uncertainty even about the fate of the human race. The Cold War added tremendously to the worries of the youth, in particular. The writer, Henry Miller stated this paradox:

> Never has there been a world so avid for security, and never has life been more insecure. To protect ourselves, we invent the most fantastic instruments of destruction, which prove to be boomerangs. No one seems to believe in the power of love, the only dependable power. No one believes in his neighbor, or in himself, let alone a supreme being. Fear, envy, suspicion are rampant everywhere. (Tytell, 7)

William Styron, another well-recognized 20th century writer, stated that his generation of the 1950s, "was not only not intact, it had in many places been cut to pieces" (Tytell, 8) and went on to say:

> We were traumatized not only by what we had been through and by the almost unimaginable presence of the bomb, but by the realization that the entire mess was not finished after all: there was now the Cold War to face, and its clammy presence oozed into our nights and days. (Tytell, 8)

The 1950s were referred to as a vacuous age. Its "citizens were generally encouraged to think well of their country" (Baym, 1763), but for the Beats, the faith in humanity that had once existed was lost. Jack Kerouac's struggle and search to find answers and his attempts to make some sense of the world directly reflect this lost faith. The Beats' belief in art as a medium of unscrambling the madness seemed all that was left, and sometimes even art was not enough. The emergence of the Beat Generation, with its new literary tenets, was practically unavoidable. Under the circumstances, it was just a matter of time before a generation such as theirs emerged and, consequently, fully embraced by the youth in the country. Jack Kerouac, then and now considered the prose laureate of the movement, was just one of many writers who expressed his feelings of loss and growing discontent. To understand Jack Kerouac and his large body of writing, we must briefly examine some of the major writers who served as his progenitors and laid some of the foundations on which he would build. We can see examples of the forces creating and fueling this angst by briefly discussing the experimental writings of T. S. Eliot, Ernest Hemingway, and James Joyce.

T. S. Eliot's writings, to some extent, focused on the social decay he saw in the time period beginning with World War I and continuing into the middle of the twentieth century. He directly criticized society and humanity in his famous poem, "The Waste Land," and he used many of the modernist characteristics of fragmentation, somehow putting the sections of the poem together to form one larger piece. Eliot used intricate fragments and violated many of the then-existing literary tenets: "The long, fragmented structure of the 'Waste Land,' too, contained so many technical innovations that ideas of what poetry was and how it worked seemed fundamentally changed. A generation of poets either imitated or resisted it" (Baym, 1258). Many readers saw the piece that appeared in 1922 as the definitive cultural statement of its time, and it reflected Eliot's fear of the destructive warfare seen in World War I. "The Waste Land" is Eliot's criticism of modern society and humanity in general. The poem is important because of the statements it makes about humanity, but its style should not be overlooked. Its modernist style reflects a discontentment with the existing rules of poetry, and Eliot made the conscious decision to violate all of these rules. The poem is composed of five "discontinuous segments, each composed of fragments incorporating multiple voices and characters, literary and historical allusions, bits and pieces of contemporary life, myths and legends" (Baym, 1259).

The restlessness of twentieth century also affected another important writer. Ernest Hemingway showed his displeasure with America when, in the 1920s, he became an expatriate and traveled overseas to Paris to join other writers, such as Gertrude Stein, Sherwood Anderson, Ezra Pound, and F. Scott Fitzgerald. As a sort of prelude to Kerouac and the Beats, Hemingway's disenchantment with America's violent involvement in the war and his criticism of a society infested with crime, danger, and violence are reflected in his first book of short stories, *In Our Time*, published in the United States in 1925. Hemingway's literary, cultural, and social importance comes from his criticisms that "portray the world of adulthood as an arena of danger and violence" (Baym, 1633). *The Sun Also Rises*, which appeared in 1926, "contrasts the empty search for sensation for a group of English and American expatriates in Paris with the rich tradition of peasant life in Spain" (Baym, 1634). In this novel, the characters cannot return to the simplicity they envy so much in the peasants because they are too self-aware and too knowledgeable: "the best they can do is develop a code by which to live with dignity and grace, while playing an unwinnable game" (Baym, 1634). Hemingway did not see American society as glorious, and certainly not sacred, as so many other Americans did at the time. Instead, Hemingway saw a society that was empty and a world that was hopeless. For him, mankind's struggle to find any meaning and order in the world was hopeless; and

Hemingway was one of many writers who most typified the angst of early to mid-twentieth century.

Finally, the writings of James Joyce also reflected a feeling of angst, and it was his style that most reflects the disenchantment that influenced Jack Kerouac. Joyce's best-known contribution to modern literature was the "stream of consciousness" technique, influential not only because it allows the reader apparent access to the very workings of a character's mind but also because, in its rejection of orthodox sentence structure and logical transition, it reminds us that literary texts achieve their most realistic effects only by manipulating language; a theme especially favored by postmodernist writers who make such functionality their chief concern (Mack, 1543).

Joyce's stream of consciousness technique sought to break established rules of proper, formal literature, and instead tried to discover new forms, which might prove to be more effective and liberating. James Joyce was the first artist to write critically about revelatory meanings which he called "epiphanies"—moments "when everything fuses and makes sense in a larger perspective" (Mack, 1544). Joyce's writing fused past and present, combined reality and imagination, and his writings during the 1920s and 1930s influenced the lives of many of his contemporaries and countless writers that followed. Joyce's techniques reflected angst by refusing to follow established rules of writing; accordingly, these techniques had a profound influence on literature of the twentieth century.

T. S. Eliot, Ernest Hemingway, and James Joyce all searched for new techniques and styles of writing, and all were successful in creating new art forms. Their works reflect both the disillusionment they experienced in the first part of the twentieth century as well as their triumph over it through art. Their influence can be seen in the works of most of the writers who were born during or after this time period.

Chapter 2

Kerouac's Young Life: Gerard, Thomas Wolfe, and Columbia University

The Beat Movement is considered by many literary critics as one of the most daring, experimental, and controversial literary movements of the twentieth century because writers associated with the Beat Movement experimented broadly with both subject matter and technique. The movement began in the late 1940s and early 1950s, but its roots actually stem, to some degree, from the tenets of Transcendentalism as well from writers mentioned in the first chapter of this book. Jack Kerouac is often seen as the most significant figure of this group of literary innovators, as he, in his plethora of essentially autobiographical books, most completely embodied the beliefs and the spirit of the movement. His books serve as personal, detailed, philosophical diaries (or accounts) of the events, experiences, and discoveries he made in his brief, but active life. They also reveal his attitudes and thoughts. Kerouac's chief activity, his struggle to find an epiphany, takes on many forms throughout his works, and each individual experience he has leads to a discovery or realization of some sort. His search for an epiphany is significant and worthy of careful study, examination, and analysis.

Kerouac's search for an epiphany, as revealed in his writings, was a complex, developing struggle that is, at first something he simply attempts to understand, albeit broadly; later, this struggle is something he actively wrestles with as presented in the ideas and answers he formulated; and, finally, his search is something he patiently, consciously, and spiritually endeavors to find in epiphanies. He defined these epiphanies as illuminations, what he referred to as, "in effect, a *satori*: the Japanese word for 'sudden illumination', 'sudden awakening', or simply a 'kick in the eye'" (Kerouac, *Satori*, 7). According to the philosophies of Confucianism and Taoism, the stated aim of Zen is none other than the aim of the Indian Buddha himself, the attainment of an absolute or ultimate knowledge lying beyond all change and the "saw of the opposites" (Ross). The state of consciousness, known in the Zen vocabulary as *satori*, is considered comparable to that special level of insight attained by Buddha while seated in deep meditation under the sacred Tree of Enlightenment in the sixth century before the birth of Christ. Zen is firmly grounded in specific exhortations of the Buddha, notably his trenchant suggestion, "Look within, thou art the Buddha" and his deathbed injunction to his disciples, "Be a lamp unto yourselves. ... Work out your own salvation with diligence" (Ross, 140).

Kerouac's books written after 1954 show a conscious reflection of and influence by the Zen Buddhism texts he was reading, and it is at this point that this idea of *satori* begins to apply more to his life and work. But his search for answers actually began at a very early age. His books written before the mid-1950s also reflect a search (albeit more haphazard) because he was looking for answers, particularly in the physical world.

Kerouac's compulsive and constant need to search, vividly captured in his books, led him to discoveries that develop in complexity with each successive book; discoveries that occur and reoccur in different forms, cumulatively linking his individual books into one magnum opus. In his writings, Kerouac tenaciously attempts to make some useful sense of the world around him.

He tries to comprehend the roles of family, the relationships of friends and lovers, the nature of love itself, and of life, solitude, recklessness, death, nature, religion, God, and a multitude of other ideas. He even attempts to discover the role that dreams play in daily life. His life story, as revealed in his works, is a fascinating tale of continuous self-discovery and incessant searching.

Lucien Carr, one of Allen Ginsberg's closest friends in college at Columbia, stated that Jack Kerouac, as well as other members of the Beat Generation tried "to look at the world in a new light, trying to look at the world in a way that gave it some meaning" (Charters, *Beat Reader*, XVIII). Kerouac's searches took him across America, and into Mexico and Europe, and, at the same time and more importantly, eventually led him inward to a probing examination of his mind, heart, and soul. The record of his searches in the works he left behind is a rich experience recorded for others to share.

This study will attempt to trace the development and evolution of Kerouac's epiphanies by first describing and listing the form in which they initially appear, then comparing them to their later reappearances, which reveal both major and minor variations. In doing so, I give attention to the stylistic features in what Kerouac himself called "spontaneous prose, a method of an 'undisturbed flow' of words from the mind onto the paper" (Donaldson, 531). Kerouac worked diligently and deliberately with this method, allowing the reader to enter his own mind, heart, and soul. This stylistic feature in Kerouac's language use proves to be linguistically and artistically liberating, contributing significantly to the level of analysis of this theme of epiphany, and is addressed in this book.

To begin this discussion, we examine the intellectual forces active with (and in) the life of Jack Kerouac. From the time Kerouac was born, on March 12, 1922, the state of the world, and more importantly, the state of American society, was changing. Historically, the decade of the 1920s in America is labeled the Jazz Age. The Roaring Twenties were a time of flappers and of extravagant consumerism, all in the aftermath of World War I. America's victory in the war created prosperity and a feeling of optimism for many U.S. citizens, but the massive destruction and countless lives lost in Europe also created a feeling of fear and horror at humanity's apparent loss of appreciation of and value for life. As irrelevant and distant as these general events may seem to be in the life of Jack Kerouac, they must not be ignored, for we will find that these events serve as a large shadow that loomed over him, as well as over the lives of all Americans of the period (either directly or indirectly).

To understand Kerouac's writings, we must also understand his life because reality and imagination are inextricably intermixed in his texts. It is important to understand that what gives the most strength to Kerouac's writing is, arguably, his ability to paint verbal descriptions of the events he experienced; descriptions of sharp clarity and artistic phrasing that show sincerity and reveal a powerful mastery of the English language.

Jack Kerouac was born in Lowell, Massachusetts, in 1922, to an immigrant French-Canadian family. His parents, Leo and Gabrielle, were honest, hard-working, simple people, and they make an appearance in nearly every one of Kerouac's books. Their influence on Jack was profoundly significant in his early years, and the examples they set for him were of courage, support, and love. His mother was devoted to the Catholic Church, but his father did not feel any sense of lasting spiritual peace (Nicosia, 24). Not only was there no solace for Leo anywhere, but he strongly disliked the church and felt it was nothing more than a money-making enterprise. Because he was very difficult to work with, his father lost his job many times. He did not like to take orders from

anyone and preferred to do things his own way. Leo Kerouac's resistance
to the Church combined with his mother's devotion to it gave Jack mixed
messages of what he should do and what he should believe. Although
Jack's parents had a great love for each other, they never quite agreed on
their religious convictions and never came to any kind of consensus. The
significance of this conflict and the impression it made on Kerouac's life
would appear in his first published novel, *The Town and the City*, which
was written between 1946 and 1949 and published in 1950. Some critics
believe that *The Town and the City* was Kerouac's way of reexamining
the complex relationship he had with his father (Nicosia, 184), a theory
which will be discussed later in this book.

Kerouac was extremely introverted as a youngster and made no friends
in the neighborhood he grew up in; indeed, if it had not been for his older
brother Gerard, he probably would have stayed in his room all day. Gerard
was extremely significant and influential in Kerouac's young life and, just
like Kerouac's parents, Gerard also appears numerous times in Kerouac's
books. Gerard's death, caused by rheumatic fever when he was only nine,
left the four-year-old Jack even more confused about life and death, and
caused him to wonder and deeply contemplate the meaning of life. Thirty
years later, Kerouac would write an autobiographical book he titled *Visions
of Gerard*, published in 1958, in which he attempts to carefully and fully
explain the significance his brother had on his own life and also attempts
to explain and affirm the impact his brother made in this world. In it,
Kerouac carefully recalls the immensely strong impression his brother's
death had on him and his life. To some extent, writing this book allowed
Kerouac to come to terms with his brother's death.

As Gerard approached death, he grew increasingly tranquil. He would
feed hungry neighbor children and explain the importance of kindness to
four-year-old "Jackie" as if Jackie were his mental equal. According to Gerald
Nicosia, author of *Memory Babe: A Critical Biography of Jack Kerouac* (1983),
Gerard unequivocally taught Jack all about the importance of a spiritual and
saintly life (26). When Jack first heard of Gerard's death, thinking it some
special good news, he gleefully ran to tell his father, who gently reprimanded
him. That may well have been the beginning of Jack's guilt over Gerard's
death, a guilt that would be problematic all of his life.

Gerard's death was an extremely pivotal event in Kerouac's young life;
the orientation, guidance, and companionship that his brother had provided

were now gone. And although Jack still had an older sister, he began living like an only child. During the day, he would play whole baseball games by himself or run horse races simply with marbles, recording their results in his own newspapers; or he would act out his own "movies" to Victrola music, then write and illustrate them in notebooks. Kerouac thus began pondering on the meaning of life when he was just a boy; his sense of quest and his search for answers were habits that began at a very early age. Additionally, Kerouac was already experiencing moments of epiphany at this early age, but to him these moments came, as they do to all children, when he experienced something new that he did not quite understand. Gerald Nicosia describes how throughout much of his life Kerouac often experienced nightmares of the night of his brother's death (Nicosia, 29). Nicosia describes in detail how his brother's death made Kerouac think often about the idea of mortality, both his own and that of his parents (Nicosia, 29).

Kerouac's formal education began at the St. Louis de France Parochial School in Centralville in the town of Lowell, Massachusetts. There, Kerouac was a good student, but the young Kerouac was also confused because the same nuns who had been at his brother's funeral, who had cried and prayed with such love and sincerity, frequently spanked him and scolded him. Kerouac's confusion about the church increased and the role it played was seen as two-sided: pious, yet strict and militant.

Due to relocation after his father's loss of a job, Kerouac then entered another school. He began attending St. Joseph's Parochial School in fifth grade, where he emerged as one of the top students. Kerouac also met another highly intelligent boy there named Arthur Louis Eno, who was very much like himself, and looked so much like Gerard that Jack, as he later recalled, immediately struck up a friendship with him (Nicosia, 31, 32).

During this time, the young Kerouac was impressionable and more spiritual than other children his age. Equally important, we can see that Gerard's influence and companionship was something young Jack was trying to replace.

It was not until Jack was nearly ten that he was able to control his sorrow. He had begun reading for hours at a time the year before, and many of his cousins and friends described him as an introverted, "different" kind of child. His avid reading combined with his father's job printing programs at the Royal Theatre, which allowed Jack to see as many free movies as he wanted, let Kerouac create a fictional world for himself that *he* could control. He would write small novels about fictional characters he imagined, and combine them with the notes he took in his spiral in which he would describe everything he saw (Nicosia, 32). His fifth grade librarian, Miss Mansfield, organized a "Scribblers' Club," and remembers that Kerouac's writing was a brilliant example of powerful and very effective descriptions (Nicosia, 32).

The young Kerouac was coming of age and his awareness of the world around him was increasing. During his junior year of high school, he was finding a great deal of intellectual excitement in the library, and there he became close friends with a very bright young boy close to his own age, John MacDonald. John had amassed and catalogued books ranging from the Greek philosophers through Shakespeare to the novels of James Joyce and D. H. Lawrence. He and Jack spent a great deal of time at each other's houses and went on long walks together (Nicosia, 33).

There was also enough drama around Kerouac to serve as material for his first writing endeavors. At home, he would hear of his father's latest adventures at the race track, for the old man was always trying out new betting systems at the horse races, which he loved passionately (Nicosia, 32, 33).

Although Kerouac's surroundings provided him outlets for learning and entertainment, he was far from secure. The outside world also showed him some of the unpleasant realities of life. One day, young Jack witnessed the sight of a man suffering a heart attack on the Moody Street Bridge, and later that same night he heard the cries of a neighbor having a seizure (Nicosia, 111). These images sent Jack trembling to the comfort of his mother's bed. Even his mother's job toiling in a shoe mill all day made him think about how life could be dictated by circumstances and how, if he himself did not control his own life, he too might end up slipping into a system of living that controlled him.

Kerouac was becoming a thoughtful adolescent in Lowell. Although the strong influence of his parochial schooling has already been mentioned, Harry Russell Huebel, a former professor of English at Texas A&I University, argues in a short biography of Kerouac that "another critical influence on Kerouac was the popular culture of the twenties and thirties. More than his family or his Catholic schooling, pop culture provided him with his earliest notions about America" (Huebel, 6). This strong influence can be seen in Kerouac's attraction to New York City and the glamorous lifestyle he hoped to someday lead as a writer.

By the time he started classes at Lowell High School, Kerouac already had his parents' lessons deeply ingrained in his psyche. His parents believed that because of his academic achievements, their son could be an example of "the American Dream" becoming a reality. Unfortunately, however, they wanted Jack to succeed according to their own definition of success, which was to gather more wealth and esteem than one's neighbors. To complicate matters, Jack's sister Caroline married at eighteen, and Jack's parents pinned all their hopes on the young boy.

But Jack was already beginning what would result in a lifelong search for knowledge. By the time Jack started high school he was already determined to be a writer. It was at this age that he began reading most avidly; the list of books read includes many of the *Harvard Classics*, the works of Johann Wolfgang von Goethe, and William Penn's *Maxims*. He also read the works of Jack London and Thomas Wolfe whose "emphasis upon the unity of their raw experiences and the creative impulse struck chords in Kerouac's sensibility" (Huebel 6, 7). Kerouac also developed a romantic image of the writer from popular culture, and after his early days in high school, Kerouac wrote "regularly (some might say obsessively) for the rest of his life" (Huebel, 7).

Kerouac would sometimes skip school and spend the day at the public library reading obsessively and voraciously. He spent countless hours devouring the works of the great minds, and he determined, more than ever, that he was going to be a writer (Nicosia, 45). When he did attend school, he rarely talked, seldom smiled, and almost never laughed, although many students felt curiosity if not actual kindness toward him. There were also many girls who had crushes on him, but he largely ignored them (Nicosia, 51).

While all of this maturing of identity and personality was taking place, Kerouac was also running track, playing football and baseball, and, incredibly, was excelling at every sport he played. His natural talent at football would later allow him to enter Columbia University with the help of a scholarship. In his baseball games, Kerouac would either hit the ball a mile or not at all; in his football games, he was known to score three or four touchdowns per quarter, making him immediately a popular student at Lowell High School both with the coaches and with the girls; and in track, he was said to have run and run until his legs hurt too much, forcing him to finally stop due to excruciating pain in his legs (Nicosia, 97).

In addition to his athletic activities, Kerouac also submitted several short stories to a contest sponsored by the school literary magazine, and one of his friends and fellow teammates at the time, Charlie Ruiter, could not help being amused by how badly Jack wished to win. Kerouac's idea of the American writer was at first idealized as a life of popularity, money, and fame, but he also idealized the beauty and the simplicity of traveling across America and seeing all of its common, working people (Nicosia, 51).

Kerouac's youth was filled with experiences not only of the Great Depression, but with the horrible news of the effects of World War II. On the very day Jack Kerouac turned sixteen, March 12, 1938, Germany was beginning its invasion of Austria, and in the months to come Adolf Hitler's armies would invade Czechoslovakia (Nicosia, 58).

The complexities of World War II grew greater than the complexities of any war or any event before it, and its effects, in one way or another, would traumatize the lives of hundreds of millions of people around the world.

For Kerouac, these war years served as a time when he began to question the nature of success. He also began an examination of the world around him and saw incredible cruelty and horror, which was magnified by his own personal visions of horror: poverty, the disintegration of his family, his father's breakdown in health, and his own personal failure to be the popular hero he had always wanted to be. Gerald Nicosia explains how all of these events absolutely overwhelmed Jack Kerouac's mind and spirit (Nicosia, 58).

As a final preparation before entering Columbia University in 1940, Jack left Lowell in 1939 to attend Horace Mann Preparatory School in New York, and there he found an entirely new world that made him realize that he had not even begun to examine his own life and his relationship with the people of the world. He also realized that he had not begun to examine the sense he had of himself as an artist and that there was yet to occur a complex opening and growth of his mind. A completely new era of his life was about to begin.

Jack was staying with his step-grandmother in New York and would ride the subway for two-and-a-half hours to Horace Mann, and after a full day of classes and football practice, he would ride the subway home for another grueling two-and-a-half hours. Kerouac began studying on the subway to take advantage of his time, but he soon found his textbooks less interesting than the faces around him.

One day, instead of going to Horace Mann, Jack decided to get off at Times Square. There he saw, for the first time in his life, the masses of the working poor and the marginalized members of society (Nicosia, 60). Kerouac instantly became aware of all the potential "learning" he could do at Times Square just by observing the countless faces living their day-to-day lives, each in their own different way. These new experiences and sights he observed at Times Square would serve as the beginning of the complex and richly dynamic developmental life Jack was destined to live.

At the age of seventeen, Kerouac began this early period of searching, which can be understood as an external, outward search in the physical world. Young Kerouac was a new arrival to New York City from the small town of Lowell, Massachusetts, and was immediately attracted to the tall buildings, the shimmering lights, and the mad hustle and bustle of city life. His privileged new friends at Horace Mann introduced him to the fast-paced life in the big city and showed him what life was like for the wealthy and elite in society. Kerouac was curious about his new friends and their way of life, yet he felt torn between his small-town lifestyle and this big city living. He was hoping to have the best of both worlds, but for the first couple of years, he was periodically debating whether he should stay and explore more of the city, or go back home and reacquaint himself with the conservative values his parents had taught him and hoped he would never abandon.

Kerouac began visiting jazz clubs with his classmates, and what attracted him most were the quick-moving tempos, the experimental rhythms, and the musical spontaneity (Nicosia, 65) that jazz music used. Kerouac wanted to learn everything about this spontaneous new sound and its sources, and the jazz players he saw every night became a very significant influence on him and his art, making him aware of the nuances of music and its similarity to the nuances of language (Nicosia, 66, 67). He was amazed at the soloists' perfect control of the instrument because the players seemed so innovative and fluid.

It was during one of his visits to a jazz club in Harlem that the eighteen-year-old Kerouac first smoked marijuana and likely tried Benzedrine as well. Kerouac was now doing crazy, reckless, experimental things that he would never have done back in Lowell. He was also growing intellectually, and his personal worldview was changing and clarifying itself.

Kerouac's writing also reflected a changing worldview. His writing at this time demonstrates numerous experiments with various themes. For example, his detective story titled "The Brothers," which is set in a big city, involves a murder mystery and makes many references to home and the beauty and peace his characters found at home (Nicosia, 67). A second story titled *"Une Veil le de Noel,"* (translated as "Christmas Eve") published in 1940, when Kerouac was only eighteen years old, contains a great deal of variation and is probably one of the first pieces that shows the influence of jazz's spontaneity. It is important to note that in these early pieces by Kerouac we get a glimpse of many of his later stylistic developments. In these early works, he also experiments with the style of writing that he would develop and eventually name "spontaneous prose," which allowed him to produce some of his most brilliant literature, and he also begins to pay close attention to details and explanations of how he uses characterization. Even in themes, Kerouac begins to develop ideas he would later explore with more significant depth and complexity. There is no doubt that at the age of eighteen, Jack Kerouac was ambitiously attempting to be new and original (Nicosia, 68).

It was also at this time that the influence of Jack London and Thomas Wolfe made its most significant impact. Jack London was a rugged adventurer who recorded many of his adventures while concurrently experiencing them and gave Jack the model for his own literary career. Thomas Wolfe also influenced him with his style of writing in which he would examine the least significant of events and explore them with deep thoughts that went to the core of not only the situation, but to the core of existence and its mystery.

While still at Horace Mann Preparatory School, Kerouac met a small literary circle of friends who called themselves "the Young Prometheans," for they were dedicated to using the power of their minds for the betterment of mankind, and it did not take long for an idealist like Kerouac to join them (Nicosia, 71). Kerouac's main goal while in this literary circle was to try and understand the world that he loved dearly. He started spending time at cafés and began reading more Thomas Wolfe as well as the works of Henry David Thoreau. He even contemplated the idea of living in the woods, but the importance his parents had placed on getting a college education made him decide against that idea.

It is important to underscore the idea that when Jack went back to his hometown of Lowell and saw his friends, he felt like he was two different individuals: he was "big-city Jack" when in New York and "Lowell Jack" when at home visiting his parents. He realized that his two groups of friends would never like each other because his Lowell friends were more concerned with settling down and getting married, as opposed to his New York friends who were more concerned with experiencing and experimenting with everything that life had to offer. The only overlap was that both groups considered Kerouac an individual who was full of humility and love.

Kerouac's writing was also already undergoing changes, not only in its experimentation with style and subject matter, but also in the fact that he began to affirm pride in his work, even though his friends were already complaining that his prose was not clear or concise, and lacked coherence (Nicosia, 84). One time Kerouac wrote a story about a gray-bearded old man in flowing white robes preaching in Times Square about the idea of the redemption of souls. Over and over the "prophet" spoke of the danger of men losing "their immortal souls," and although his friends told him the story had no plot, Kerouac was very proud of it. One friend named George Murray told him it was "interesting" and was extremely surprised when Kerouac told him to keep it as a gift. George refused and advised him to keep work like this for himself.

Jack's circle of friends almost never talked about religion, although he was getting deeply involved in his own private debate over religion and the place it had in his own life. He was living a simple but wholesome life at the time. But his readings of Spengler's book *The Decline of the West* and some James Joyce material, coupled with regular beer-drinking conversations with his close literary circle was forming the foundations on which Kerouac would build his personal and literary life. When he read James Joyce's *Ulysses*, Jack was amazed at the discipline and deliberateness that had gone into producing the illusion of stream of consciousness and found an influence, a model, and a mentor in Joyce's work.

Three months later, in 1942, Kerouac enrolled at Columbia, and his father started telling him that he had become too rebellious and somewhat of a truant and a hoodlum (Nicosia, 106). Kerouac was strongly pursuing any and every capricious interest he had and was drinking whiskey heavily. Additionally, he was now in and out of relationships regularly and became just as careless with the jobs he had. He was also losing his shyness and the humility his friends had once admired. He neglected his homework and would instead go to Harlem to visit and talk to Jazz musicians, asking them to share their experiences and secrets in creating their music. He also began taking Benzedrine more regularly and began smoking marijuana more regularly as well. His girlfriend at the time, Edie Parker, was sometimes terrified that Jack was going to lose his talent as a writer in the pursuit of new experiences.

At this early age, Kerouac already foresaw as his life's work the creation of a contemporary historical record in which style would play a subordinate role and what was to be privileged was absolute fidelity to the events and thoughts that registered in his consciousness (Nicosia, 109). Kerouac moved in with Edie in her new apartment at 421 West 118th Street, and here Kerouac found not only true love for a woman, but he also found tender encouragement for his writing. During intimate conversations, Jack often told Edie about the sadness left in him by Gerard's death. Kerouac would end up marrying Edie Parker in 1944, but their marriage ended in divorce within a few months.

In early 1944, Jack also found a supportive group of friends who would influence and encourage him to write the many stories he wished to write. Edie's curiosity and flirtatiousness with other men led to Jack's meeting with Lucien Carr, an art student at Columbia. Carr was immediately captivated by Kerouac's warmth and by how "each person who came into Jack's life was someone for Kerouac to love" (Dardess, 287). Carr soon brought a new friend to Edie's apartment, the then-seventeen-year-old poet Allen Ginsberg. Ginsberg had already heard about Kerouac and admired him as a mature writer, and Ginsberg's honesty and experiences were things that Kerouac quickly became strongly interested in; they soon formed a close friendship that was not only strongly rooted in literature and poetry, but also in a love and passion and willingness to experience everything that life had to offer. "Both young men were united by their spirituality, their love of poetry, and their maturing sense of the destructiveness of the modern industrial state" (Dardess, 284).

One day, a friend of Carr's walked in with a tall, slim St. Louis aristocrat and Harvard graduate, William Burroughs. Burroughs had come looking for Kerouac because he wanted to get some information about joining the Merchant Marines, an outfit Jack had been enlisted in and travelled with a couple of months earlier. Kerouac was extremely drawn to Burroughs's intelligence and experiences as well as his interest and experimentalism in his own writings.

Soon, Kerouac's new group of friends were introducing him to the works of Rimbaud, Baudelaire, Nietzsche, and many others, and Burroughs's explanations and instruction through these literary works drew respect from both Kerouac and Ginsberg. The works Kerouac and his friends liked most were the ones that were most stylistically and thematically unconventional (Nicosia, 120). The readings and discussions of these texts led to another of Kerouac's self-analytical phases, although the price he paid for it was significant: since he had continually skipped classes at Columbia and had stopped going to football practice, the head coach decided to cut Kerouac from the team, which terminated his football scholarship as well. Kerouac's parents were tremendously disappointed because they had had their hearts set on him getting a college education and had much faith in their son, but they were even more upset with Jack's new liberated, careless, bohemian lifestyle. His father was direct with his criticisms about how his girlfriend was a tramp and how his friends were lazy and should try to get real jobs (Nicosia, 123). His mother was not as critical, but she was upset that her son had lost and forgotten so many of his values. Despite all this condemnation, Jack was already focused on becoming the best writer he could become, and defined his mission as "self- ultimacy"; this included the creation of a new "artistic morality" (Dardess, 284). Jack was twenty-two now, and with his newly acquired intellectual independence, he was about to begin actively pursuing answers to his many varied questions about the meaning of life.

Chapter 3

Kerouac's Search Begins: The Town and the City *and* the Martin Family

This leads us to a more crystalized and first identifiable stage of the search for an epiphany in Jack Kerouac's life, which is marked by new preoccupations, interests, and themes. This first stage can be described as an honest attempt to pursue answers in the outside world and shows Kerouac experimenting not only with different lifestyles and relationships he has with friends and lovers, but he also begins to show the spiritual and religious dimensions of his searches that will develop and grow in both depth and complexity as Jack's life and search both continue.

Many biographers believe Kerouac's liberation came when his father, Leo Kerouac, finally died of stomach cancer. Jack had been nursing his sick father for nearly seven months between 1945 and 1946. Kerouac felt guilty about writing anything during this time he was at home because his mother was working at a shoe mill, and his father was too tired and sick to work; he felt that his main responsibility was to look after his father. When his father died in May of 1946, Kerouac immediately began his work on *The Town and the City*, which was to be published four years later in 1950:

> The theme of the book was based most directly on Kerouac's recent experience of the split between his parents and his friends. But in this split Kerouac saw a more general division between his hometown, with its traditional social and religious values, and the city, with its intellectual stimulations and physical dangers. He further observed that the split was psychological as well as social since each side of the split was but a part of the whole, and by itself insufficient to satisfy the heart and mind. The town, for all its snug attractiveness, had become merely confining, while the city, for all its promises of limitless freedom, had become destructive, since no limits on behavior were permitted. (Dardess, 285)

Excerpts from George Dardess, *The Beats: Literary Bohemians in Postwar America*, ed. Ann Charters. Copyright © 1983 by Cengage Learning, Inc.

The Town and the City is Kerouac's first serious attempt to make some sense of the world around him and to find some kind of balance and understanding of not only the town and the city, but it also attempts to find a balance between feeling alive versus feeling like he was simply existing. Kerouac believed that nothing was certain in this world, and everything was always at war with its extreme. Even "God's presence was at once close and infinitely distant, reliable and unpredictable, undeservedly rewarding and punishing, blissful and painful" (Dardess, 286), and Kerouac wanted to come to some understanding of and about God and His mysterious ways. Among Kerouac's themes that appear in some manifestation or another throughout his many publications, one of the greatest of them is that his books represent a tireless effort to make sense of these apparent discontinuities between God's presence and absence in matter, behavior, imagination, and thought (Dardess, 286).

Kerouac wrote most of *The Town and the City* in several sittings between 1946 and 1949. At this time, Kerouac had already taken to the road, and constant travel led back and forth across the country with his new, and extremely influential friend, Neal Cassady. The influence Cassady had on Kerouac not only affected his life and the material in his writings, but it also gave him an entirely new world view as well as a new vision of himself as a writer. In *The Town and the City*, Cassady plays a minor, yet significant and influential role, and although some of the adventures he and Neal Cassady experienced are described, Kerouac primarily struggles with his own search for answers and meanings, and it is his own life that is examined. This book is an extremely valuable in providing insights into Kerouac's early preoccupations, beliefs, searches, answers, and talents as a young writer.

It is important to mention that although Jack Kerouac had already been writing seriously for nearly ten years, he admits to modeling his style in *The Town and the City* after that of Thomas Wolfe. In his own books, Wolfe talks about "cosmic moments" and has "epiphanies about timelessness that are presented through a series of precise perceptions" (Nicosia, 304). Kerouac attempts to duplicate these "epiphanies about timelessness …" and builds upon Wolfe's ideals using his own style. The style of Thomas Wolfe can clearly be seen in Kerouac's long, expansive, wide-ranging, and far-reaching paragraphs that strive to get at deeper meanings and understandings of some of the mysteries of life. In *Look Homeward, Angel*, the main character, Eugene Gant, sees himself as a social misfit and leaves his family to attend college.

When he comes back, he feels like a changed person who is out of touch with his family. The character tries to make sense of the feelings of loneliness he has and concludes that life in this world is a very sad experience. Kerouac imitates not only Wolfe's themes, but also employs Wolfe's style. Kerouac's long sentences and paragraphs are largely based on Wolfe's style, and what Kerouac's characters ascertain in his own book is extremely important and shows a mature mind at work.

In *The Town and the City* Kerouac also uses language in a way to allow the many thoughts in his mind to roll onto the text. Very much like James Joyce, Kerouac uses a stream of consciousness technique mostly in his language, although not necessarily in the storyline and plot. The plot itself is rather coherent and tightly organized. Kerouac would perfect this style of writing called "spontaneous prose" in subsequent books, but already, Kerouac's sentence structure and paragraph structure show some experimentation:

> When all the family was stilled in sleep, when the streetlamp a few paces from the house shone at night and made grotesque shadows of the trees upon the house, when the river sighed off in the darkness, when the trains hooted on their way to Montreal far upriver, when the wind swished in the soft tree leaves and something knocked and rattled on the old barn you could stand in old Galloway Road and look at this home and know that there is nothing more haunting than a house at night when the family is asleep, something strangely tragic, something beautiful forever. (Kerouac, *The Town and the City*, 7)

In this first novel, Kerouac writes about The Martin family, a family of eleven, living in the small town of Galloway, near The Merrimack River in the New Hampshire Hills. Kerouac records the rupture of the family caused by World War II and by the decisions each member has to make when entering the adult world. He then follows through with the effects of the decisions each individual makes and tries to make sense of these effects to unify the storyline. Although the novel is largely based on events in Kerouac's own life, it is not directly autobiographical: "He distributes aspects of his own personality among the various children of the family and adjusts the facts of his life to give the story internal coherence" (Dardess, 286).

The sample passage above shows that Kerouac was already experimenting with style, and these long, rambling one-sentence paragraphs

Excerpts from Jack Kerouac, *The Town and the City*. Copyright © 1978 by Houghton Mifflin Harcourt.

appear ubiquitously throughout the novel. Kerouac submitted a 1,200-page manuscript to Harcourt Brace and was asked to revise and edit the novel. The result was a 500-page published novel. Kerouac's tireless efforts to make sense of the world around him and to find answers for his search reveal epiphanies that are both well thought out and explained, while others he stumbles over accidentally.

Kerouac tells us in the beginning of the book,

> This is the Martin family, the elders and the young ones, even the little ones, the flitting ghost—ends of a brood who will grow and come to attain size and seasons and huge presence like the others, and burn savagely across days and nights of living, and give brooding rare articulation to the poor things of life, and the rich, dark things too. (Kerouac, *The Town and the City*, 15)

Here, Kerouac counts every member of the family as an equal and shows confidence in the sense of quest that is experienced and shared by everyone. Kerouac addresses many themes in this first book, such as the differences between childhood and adulthood, the issue and relationship between life and death, and the concept of time and timelessness. He also addresses the tenderness and warmth that the family represents and the theme of the home and homeliness, and he even addresses, at great length, the similarities and dichotomies he sees in men and women. The result is "the apprentice work of a major novelist, flawed by an imitative and verbose style, and confused with a welter of tentative approaches, but nonetheless notable for the highly consistent symbolism Kerouac develops to deal with troubling questions like loss, sickness, and death" (Nicosia, 318, 319).

All of the characters in the novel are searching for something or are trying to comprehend their existence and their place in this world. Kerouac also seems to have an admiration for the motherly figures in this world, especially for Mrs. Martin, the mother of the nine Martin children. If we examine Kerouac's relationship with his own mother we can see in Mrs. Martin a great deal of overlap, and the conclusions Kerouac makes are incredibly poignant, insightful, and tender:

> The mother completes a chore in the kitchen, listens to the late evening news on the radio, has her cup of tea with crackers, and yawns, and tells Rosey to close the windows upstairs. To eat, and to sleep, to have a house and to live in it, to have a family and to

live with them—these are the things she knows. To bask in the days that keep coming and going, to keep the house warm and clean and enjoyable, to prepare food and eat it and store it, to conquer sickness, keep things together, preside over the sweet needs and plain satisfactions of life, and to order the furies of existence around all these things—this is what she knows, and she understands that there is nothing else to know.

The depth of a woman's heart is as unknowable as that of man's, but nothing like restlessness and feverish rue ever abides there. In the very deeps of this heart are contained all the secrets, and the one plain secret of life, which is something that is homely, coarse, sensual, and deep, something that is everlasting because it is serene and waits patiently. A man may spend the night tracing the course of the stars above the earth, but the woman never has to worry her head about the course of the stars above the earth, because she lives in the earth and the earth is her home. A man may yearn after a thousand shades and shapes that surround his fevered life, but to the woman there is only one shade and one shape to things, which she forever contemplates in the fullness of her profundity, and she never loses sight of it.

Some men dig into the earth to excavate whole lost cities and civilizations, they want to find otherworldly mysteries and strange things never known before. But if you dig into a woman's heart, "deeply beneath whatever surface it presents, the deeper you go, the more woman there is; and if you're looking for mysteries there, you'll find that they don't matter." (Kerouac, *The Town and the City*, 68, 69)

In this passage, we can see that some of Kerouac's searches and answers are targeted at universal themes, such as the differences he believes exist between men and women. The conclusions that Kerouac reaches and draws reveal a mature and serious artist at work.

Although Kerouac uses all of the characters to somehow represent himself, Peter Martin is given most of Kerouac's own qualities and bears the strongest resemblance to Kerouac himself. Peter is seventeen in the novel and goes off to college where he meets a group of artistic Bohemian friends. He goes through many periods of confusion and has adventures strikingly similar to those that Kerouac had several years before. Also like Kerouac, Peter feels out of place when he goes back home and realizes that his search for the feeling of home is now to be found in the hustle and bustle of the city, or on the road. Peter Martin does not feel at home back in his hometown. It is important to examine Kerouac's descriptions and thoughts of the character that are most closely related to himself in the novel:

> Peter went home to his family that autumn.
> A sharp knowledge had now come to him of the tragic alone-ness of existence and the need of beating it off with love and devotion instead of surrendering to it with that perverse, cruel, unnecessary self-infliction that he saw everywhere around him, that he himself had nursed for so long. (Kerouac, *The Town and the* City, 468)

Kerouac was being influenced and affected by many different individuals and ideas at the time that make this passage seem quite inconsistent with the lifestyle he was actually leading; in particular, the influence of Neal Cassady and other members of the Beat Generation, who were already experimenting frequently with drugs and alcohol. Additionally, if we examine the life that Kerouac had led during his own college years, the reader might be quite surprised to learn that the young author could write with such morality and with such personal reform.

Peter Martin is also the character that develops the most; towards the end of the novel, his moments of epiphanies are consistent with the ones he has had at the beginning, still deeply rooted in morality. The death of Peter Martin's father was one of:

> These things (that) began to work their change on young Peter who saw, as in an ancient vision spaded up from his being, what life must be about, at last. He saw that it was love and work and true hope. He saw that all the love in the world, which was sweet and fine, was not love at all without its work, and that work could not exist without the kindness of hope. (Kerouac, *The Town and the City,* 472)

Kerouac describes more of Peter's conclusions on that same page:

> He saw that all the struggles of life were incessant, laborious, painful, that nothing was done quickly, without labor, that it had to undergo a thousand fondlings, revisings, moldings, addings, removings, graftings, tearings, correctings, smoothings, rebuild-ings, reconsiderings, nailings, tackings, chippings, hammerings, hoistings, connectings—all the poor fumbling uncertain incomple-tions of human endeavor. They went on forever and were forever

> incomplete, far from perfect, refined, or smooth, full of terrible memories of failure and fears of failure, yet, in the way of things, somehow noble, complete, and shining in the end. (Kerouac, *The Town and the City*, 472)

Kerouac's words and thoughts, via Peter, reveal a very reflective, thoughtful, and philosophical worldview, and what Peter concludes in the novel is that life is a constantly growing and expanding adventure where conclusions never really replace others that have already been formulated, but instead, these conclusions only *add* additional layers to the library of experiences one has.

Although the family is dispersed because of the war, and the novel ends tragically with the death of Peter's father and youngest brother, Charlie, Kerouac still expresses, through Peter, an optimism about mankind's role in life. Kerouac seems to "regard death as the ultimate human tragedy" (Nicosia, 343), and points out how death makes no distinctions and therefore, decides to allow the death of not only the oldest person in the Martin family but also the youngest. Kerouac also makes a strong argument for hard work in life.

All of these arguments show the influence that Kerouac's parents had on his life. Although Kerouac's own father had just died, with the writing and publication of his first novel, he hoped to regain his mother's acceptance.

The Town and the City is a very impressive first novel and reveals a writer that is insightful, intelligent, and mature. It proves that Kerouac indeed knew how to write in the traditional style of the novel. Many critics who have closely read this first novel agree that Kerouac's writing ability does indeed have considerable merit. Although Kerouac went beyond the traditional novel in his later works, he never neglected first working his way through the structure and conventions of the traditional novel, at least as he understood those characteristics.

When *The Town and the City* was reviewed by *Newsweek* on March 13, 1950, Kerouac and his writing received favorable critiques:

> In many respects, John Kerouac, now 28, is the best and most promising of the young novelists whose first works have recently appeared ... *The Town and the City* is almost a major work. It is almost the fusion of warmth and emotion with the plain reality of American life that critics have asked for in American fiction. ... The story is in part the transformation of the Martin family with years and the war. There is also the transformation of the country, from

> the football-playing, back-slapping days at Galloway to the lurid
> hysteria of intellectual life in New York, with something snarling
> and savage replacing the old good nature, and with characters
> seemingly poised, when the book ends, still able to go one way
> or the other. ...
>
> Kerouac writes, overwrites, repeats himself, as did Tom
> [Thomas] Wolfe; the long-winded nonsense of his intellectuals is
> well-nigh unreadable. But his average citizens are an awesome
> group of plain people, sisters and brothers, affectionate, intense,
> high-spirited, foolish and self-centered, but with sudden insights
> and moments of tenderness that give their relationship a poignant
> loveliness. (*Newsweek*, March 13, 1950)

Although Kerouac was already actively involved in his friendships with several members of the Beat Generation such as Allen Ginsberg, William Burroughs, Neal Cassady, and John Clellon Holmes, Kerouac wrote most of the story under the strong moral influence of his parents.

In a general analysis, *The Town and the City* deals with themes such as friendship and love between simple people living simple lives. These are explained in detail and with sincere thoughtfulness, along with a depth and breadth of human understanding. The writing reveals some experimentation not only with the classic style of paragraphing and chapter divisions, but also, more importantly, it reveals Kerouac's first literary efforts to create his own unique, bold writing style.

Anyone who reads *The Town and the City* must keep in mind that the book is, to some extent, a "grief-stricken" autobiographical attempt on Kerouac's part to expunge the feelings of guilt he was having believing he had disgraced his family (specifically his father) by dropping out of Columbia and living his Bohemian lifestyle. Kerouac decided to "write a huge novel explaining everything to everybody" that he hoped would redeem him in his family's eyes (Charters, *On the Road*, XII). Kerouac hoped to create something that his family would be proud of, and, although sales were low, his mother and sister accepted the book and were ecstatic to see it published in 1950. Contrary to his own expectations, however, Kerouac did not find himself "redeemed" after he had finished writing *The Town and the City* in 1948. Instead, it initiated the next period of his life, which was his most productive period of literary works as well as the most experimental.

Chapter 4

On the Road for Seven Years, On the Road, and International Fame

In *The Town and the City*, Kerouac presents several of the themes he would later struggle with and expand upon. His previous desires of going on the road take action after this first period of his life and he becomes intent not only in seeing the America of his romantic vision, but he also devoted himself to finding answers for a way of life he could truly embrace. He also searched for a writing style that allowed him greater freedom to fully articulate what he thought and believed. Although his personal feelings of redemption were not complete after the publication of his first novel, Kerouac had gained a sense of direction and established his footing on the path he was to follow for the next seven years of his life.

The last page of *The Town and the City* establishes the groundwork that Kerouac would build upon not only in his later works, but also in his own life. Peter Martin leaves the reader with a still-questioning sense of search. At the end of the novel, Peter is hitchhiking across the country somewhere in a small town. Kerouac writes:

> Peter Martin, in his black leather jacket, carrying the old canvas bag in which all his poor needments for a long journey were packed, got down from the truck.
> And Peter was alone in the rainy night.
> He was on the road again, traveling the continent westward, going off to further years, alone by the waters of life, alone, looking towards the lights of the river's cape, towards tapers burning warmly in the towns, looking down along the shore in remembrance of the dearness of his father and of all life.
> The ... crowded treetop shores and wandering waters showed through shrouds of rain. When the railroad trains moaned, the river-winds blew, bringing echoes through the vale, it was as if a wild hum of voices, the dear voices of everybody he had known,

were crying: "Peter, Peter! Where are you going, Peter?" And a big
soft gust of rain came down.
He put up the collar of his jacket, and bowed his head, and hurried
along. (Kerouac, *The Town and the City*, 498)

Through the character of Peter, Kerouac is indirectly predicting and
foreshadowing the life on the road he is about to begin leading. At the end
of the novel, Peter comes to no absolute and final conclusions except that the
randomness of the universe is unfair and indifferent to everyone. He makes
a poignant statement about how his own life is like that of a fish that he once
saw being caught whose hook tore part of its mouth while it flittered wildly
gasping for air trying to hold on to dear life. Like Peter, Kerouac has to find
out for himself what the meaning of his own life is, and he must do this
not vicariously, but through firsthand experiences. Nothing would be taken
secondhand anymore in Kerouac's life, and this first book serves not only as
a literary, philosophical text with an attempted albeit loose resolution, but it
also initiates Kerouac's own lifelong personal search for answers and affirms
his bravery and willingness to explore and experiment.

Kerouac's strong interest in jazz music, along with his new friendships
with Allen Ginsberg and William Burroughs and his exposure to their
autobiographical narratives and poetry were leading and encouraging him
to experiment with his own style of writing. Meeting Neal Cassady, a young
Californian fresh out of reform school, strongly influenced Kerouac's decision not only to travel more extensively than he had done before, but also
to experiment with the style of writing he frequently attempts in *The Town
and the City*. This style of writing simply advocated one thing; "to honestly
confess everything from within using words" (Donaldson, 531). Kerouac
found a model for the writing he had wanted to experiment with himself
in the letters he received from Cassady, "particularly Cassady's style of
combining loose, rambling sentences with meticulously detailed observa-
tions" (Charters, XVII). Kerouac would experiment extensively with this
style after the publication of the first novel, and his struggle to find a unique
voice and style in the midst of all his literary contemporaries can be seen as a
search for an epiphany itself.

After Kerouac's second marriage to Joan Haverty in 1950, he began modeling his writing after the "kickwriting momentum" of Cassady's letters. And
when Joan asked Kerouac what he and Neal had really done during their
cross-country trips together in 1947 and 1948, Kerouac decided to write his

"road book as if telling her what had happened on the cross-country trips before their marriage, using first-person narration like that of Burroughs's autobiography but imitating Cassady's confessional style, dramatizing the emotional effect his road experiences had on him" (Charters, XIX). Kerouac was convinced that his:

> ... verbal flow was hampered when he had to change paper at the end of a page, so he taped together twelve-foot long sheets of drawing paper, trimmed at the left margin so they would fit into his typewriter, and fed them into his machine as a continuous role. John Clellon Holmes visited his apartment while this version of *On the Road* was in progress and was amazed at the thundering sound of Jack's typewriter racing non-stop.
>
> Joan had taken a job as a waitress, and when she got home she fed Jack pea soup and coffee; he took Benzedrine to stay awake. Joan was impressed by the fact that Jack sweated so profusely while writing *On the Road* that he went through several T-shirts a day. He hung the damp shirts all over the apartment so they could dry. Kerouac started his book in early April 1951. By April 9, he had written thirty-four thousand words. By April 20, eighty-six thousand. On April 27, the book was finished, a roll of paper typed as a single-spaced paragraph 120 feet long. He showed it triumphantly to Holmes, who was astonished at its appearance. Holmes remembered that Kerouac was ecstatic at having established a 'new trend in American literature.'
>
> If the writing of Holmes, Burroughs, and Cassady had given Kerouac useful models of autobiographical narrative in early 1951, his three years spent studying the work of American novelists and experimenting with form and language for his 'road book' also prepared him for his three weeks of marathon typing. Kerouac loathed Hemingway's 'sparse and halting' literary style, and he was critical of the romantic fiction of 'Scott Fitz,' but his study of *The Great Gatsby* at the New School had shown him the value of inventing a sympathetic narrator to tell the story of an American hero who fled his past to embrace what he imagined was the freedom of his future. (Charters, XIX–XX)

In 1950, Kerouac sacrificed greatly and put forth a tremendous effort in the writing of the original version of *On the Road*, which is a great deal different from the version that Viking Press published in 1957. Not only is the storyline and subject matter vibrant and action filled, but the writing

Excerpts from *The Portable Beat Reader*, ed. Ann Charters. Copyright © 1992 by Penguin Random House LLC.

style itself promotes, encourages, and facilitates the spirit of the adventures that Jack and his friends experienced.

On the Road is almost like a double epiphany in itself. Not only is Kerouac literally "on the road" searching for answers, seeing America, and exploring the West of his dreams—that land of limitless possibility—but the style in which the book was written is crucial and reveals a stylistic epiphany for Kerouac. John Clellon Holmes was a friend of Kerouac's since about the age of 25 and has written a number of essays about him. In a book published in 1958 titled *Nothing More to Declare*, one of the essays titled "The Great Rememberer," Holmes describes the Kerouac he knew in 1950, during this "middle period" of Kerouac's quest:

> I was married, and rooted in New York. I was ambitious for fame and money, and had not yet come upon my own themes. Kerouac, on the other hand, was trying to find a fate to which he could consign himself. He was trying to make a soul-choice, once and for all, between the cozy nest of love and work the boy he had once been longed to build (particularly when in revulsion against cities, and city-centerlessness), and the Wild Road of freedom and possibility to which the man he was becoming was so powerfully attracted.
>
> These were the years of his obsession with Neal Cassady (the 'Dean' or 'Cody' of the books); the Neal he had met a few years earlier, whose raw energies drew Kerouac back and forth across the continent time and time again; in whom he invested for a while all his deep, and deeply thwarted, fraternal emotions; and from whose vagabond joys and woes created his most vivid portrait of the young, rootless American, high on life. As Americans always have, Kerouac hankered for the West, for Western health and openness of spirit, for the immemorial dream of freedom, joy, communion and Oriental Oneness that even Concord-bound Thoreau always sauntered toward, and his peevish indictments of New York (and New Yorkishness) were symptomatic of his feeling that a certain reckless idealism, a special venturesomeness of heart, had been outlawed to the margins of American life in his time. His most persistent desire in those days was to chronicle what was happening on those margins. (Holmes, 75, 76)

Kerouac was searching for answers and a way of life he could live by, but he was equally searching for a style of writing that allowed him the stylistic freedom he wanted and that his adventures demanded. In *The Town and the*

Excerpts from John Clellon Holmes, *Nothing More to Declare*. Copyright © 1967 by E. P. Dutton and Co.

City Kerouac was searching for moorings in his anchorless life, but he was already "experimenting with prose methods that would allow him to break free of the slow, calculated, laborious techniques he had employed in writing his novel" (Dardess, 287). After his first novel, Kerouac felt restricted and limited with his imitation of the traditional writing style of the novel and wanted to work with a new style that would allow him the flexibility he desired.

Meeting Neal Cassady was pivotal in this artistic endeavor, and when Cassady advised him to "just write it all down the way it comes out from within" Kerouac began experimenting with the earliest forms of "spontaneous prose." Kerouac would later publish a short list of guidelines that he called "Essentials of Spontaneous Prose." In this list, he outlines some simple precepts the writer should keep in mind while writing:

> Begin not from preconceived idea of what to say about image but from jewel center of interest in subject of image at moment of writing, and write outwards swimming in sea of language to peripheral release and exhaustion—Do not after think except for poetic P.S. reasons. Never after think to improve or defray impressions, as the best writing is always the most personal wrung-out tossed from cradle warm protective mind-tap from yourself the song of yourself, blow: —now! —your way is your only way— 'good'— or 'bad' —always honest, ('ludicrous') spontaneous, 'confessional' interesting because not 'crafted.' Craft is craft. (Rpt. in Donaldson, 533)

Kerouac was experimenting tremendously with style and felt that this new technique of writing overlapped with morality. He believed that his thoughts were moral and spiritual and that they should be left untouched from how they conceptualized as a mixture of both the heart and brain. In October of 1951, Kerouac described this method as a "wild form" that moves beyond "the arbitrary confines of the story ... into realms of revealed Picture. ... Wild form's the only form holds what I have to—my mind is exploding to say something about every image and every memory ... I have an irrational lust to set down everything I know" (Charters, XXV).

John Clellon Holmes poignantly,

> ... understood that the characters in *On the Road* were actually on a quest, and that the specific object of their quest was spiritual. Though they rushed back and forth across the country on the

slightest pretext, gathering kicks along the way, their real journey
was inward; and if they seemed to trespass most boundaries, legal
and moral, it was only in the hope of finding a belief on the other
side. (Charters, XXX)

Holmes's statement seems true, but the evidence in the novel suggests
that Kerouac was at this time searching for answers primarily in the physical
world of people and places in America. Kerouac did not yet have the sense of
heightened understanding he would later develop, and although this period
also reveals Kerouac simultaneously looking inwardly at himself, he is still
primarily relying on the physical world of people and places for answers.

The hero of *On the Road*, Dean Moriarty, is a romanticized characterization of Neal Cassady, and in his description of the adventures,
Kerouac indirectly reveals his fascination with the real-life Neal Cassady.
In the early pages of the story, Kerouac, through his semi-fictional and
semi-autobiographical character, Sal Paradise, sets off alone to meet Dean
Moriarty out on the west coast, not knowing exactly where and why he
is going. He does not even know what he is chasing after, but Paradise
is hoping to get more than "kicks" from his time spent on the road. Sal
Paradise says early on: "Somewhere along the line I knew there'd be girls,
visions, everything; somewhere along the line the pearl would be handed
to me" (Kerouac, *On the Road*, 11).

This passage reveals not only Kerouac's own lack of focus and uncertainty
about what he was hoping to find when he met up with Neal Cassady, but it
also confirms that Kerouac felt he was indeed on a quest for answers. At the
beginning of the book, Sal Paradise travels alone at times on his way West
to the "Promised Land," and one night he stops in Des Moines to sleep and
describes how:

I woke up as the sun was reddening; and that was the one dis-
tinct time in my life, the strangest moment of all, when I didn't
know who I was—I was far away from home, haunted and tired
with travel, in a cheap hotel room I'd never seen, hearing the hiss
of steam outside, and the creak of the old wood of the hotel, and
footsteps upstairs, and all the sad sounds, and I looked at the
cracked high ceiling and really didn't know who I was for about
fifteen strange seconds. I wasn't scared; I was just somebody
else, some stranger, and my whole life was a haunted life, the
life of a ghost. I was halfway across America, at the dividing line
between the East of my youth and the West of my future, and

Excerpts from Jack Kerouac, *On the Road*. Copyright © 1999 by Penguin Random House LLC.
Reprinted with permission.

maybe that's why it happened right there and then, that strange red afternoon. (Kerouac, *On the Road*, 17)

Here we can see that, surprisingly, Kerouac himself was often shocked and confused with what he was actually doing on the road. We can also see him seeking a style of writing that would encompass *everything*. Kerouac seems to be acutely aware of everything going on in the world around him and pays significant attention to the most infinitesimal mental details. During this middle period of Kerouac's life, he frequently describes things as "strange" and, although he tries to clarify his adventures and search on paper, readers can still see that Kerouac was at times confused by what "everything" meant and was unclear about its actual significance and the effect it had on his life.

Sal Paradise's vision of the West as the Promised Land is very important in the novel and, although he did not know exactly what he was hoping to find, he did know he wanted to get away from New York. Later in the book, Paradise tells a girl he meets at a bus station, "Ain't nothin in New York" (Kerouac, *On the Road*, 35). His sense of the freedom and his feeling of the uncharted West allowed possibility and expression, unlike the limits placed on the individual in America's northeast. Therefore, although Paradise did not know exactly what he hoped to find in the West, he did know that he wanted to discover the freedom he believed it would allow.

Sal Paradise was also on a quest for love and a romantic relationship. He writes:

Oh where is the girl I love? I thought, and looked everywhere, as I had looked everywhere in the little world below. And before me was the great raw bulge and bulk of my American continent; somewhere far across, gloomy, crazy New York was throwing up its cloud of dust and brown steam. There is something brown and holy about the East; and California is white like wash lines and emptyheaded—at least that's what I thought then. (Kerouac, *On the Road*, 79)

Throughout the book, Sal Paradise meets different women and wonders if each one might be the true love of his life. He says, "A pain stabbed my heart, as it did every time I saw a girl I loved who was going the opposite direction in this too-big world" (Kerouac, *On the Road*, 81).

He also makes frequent references to God and the Lord throughout the novel. He writes, "I looked up at the dark sky and prayed to God for a better break in life and a better chance to do something for the little people I loved" (Kerouac, *On the Road*, 96). In numerous places, Kerouac characterizes Sal Paradise as a very giving, extremely generous person, who seems to be actively soul searching, but also, perhaps too easily influenced by those around him.

During this period of his life, while Kerouac was searching for answers in the outer world, he often wondered if he should move back to Lowell and enjoy the peaceful life that his hometown offered. Kerouac still seemed torn between the two very different worlds of his small town life and his unpredictable, apparently aimless life on the road. In *On the Road*, he makes direct references to home and to the theme and idea of home, and complains directly about the cruelties he experiences while on the road.

About a third of the way through the novel, Sal Paradise meets a Mexican field worker and her baby boy. He falls in love with her and takes a job working in the fields, postponing his reaching California and seeing his friends. This postponement is very important because Paradise's willingness to spend time with the different people he meets gives the reader an insight into the sense of his quest and reveals the fact that Kerouac, on his journey to the American West, really did want to gain wisdom. Paradise's susceptibility shows a very open-minded, inquisitive sojourner; he writes:

> Every day I earned approximately a dollar and a half. It was just enough to buy groceries in the evening on the bicycle. The days rolled by. I forgot all about the East [New York] and about Dean [Neal Cassady] and Carlo [Allen Ginsberg] and the bloody road. (Kerouac, *On the Road*, 97)

However, on the very next page of the novel Sal Paradise says, "I could feel the pull of my own life calling me back"; and he says this when he gets tired of working and picking cotton and wants to get back on the road (Kerouac, *On the Road*, 98). Paradise's decisions in the novel are like a pendulum swinging back and forth, and this pattern repeats and reappears throughout the entire text.

Eventually in the novel, the strong influence of Dean Moriarty and his aimlessness directly influences Sal Paradise. Sal Paradise is completely fascinated by Dean Moriarty and also begins looking aimlessly for what Moriarty is looking for—fun and excitement:

> Socially an outcast, Cassady (Moriarty) yet possessed a spontaneous, exuberant energy and a belief in divine power that could not

fail to make him, in Kerouac's eyes, the positive embodiment of his social criticism. Kerouac had been needing the encouragement to believe that the values which he placed his trust could take external form, and such a form had arrived. (Dardess, 288)

About halfway through the book, Sal Paradise says to Dean Moriarty and his young wife, "I want to marry a girl so I can rest my soul with her till we both get old. This can't go on all the time—all this franticness and jumping around. We've got to go someplace, find something" (Kerouac, *On the Road*, 116). Moriarty responds by saying in the next paragraph, "Ah now man, I've been digging you for years about home and marriage and all those fine wonderful things about your soul" (Kerouac, *On the Road*, 116). Kerouac makes an extremely strong and honest statement here that is authentically autobiographical. Readers can see that Sal Paradise wants to feel a *genuine sense* of home, and even Dean Moriarty recognizes this longing desire in his friend. Readers can also see that Kerouac does indeed authentically desire to reach an authentic sense of *something* on the road.

Later in the book, Sal Paradise again mentions the theme of home. As he and Dean are traveling on the road, Sal describes the "comfortable little homes with chimneys smoking and how they appeared along the road at intervals. I wished we could go in for buttermilk and beans in front of the fireplace" (Kerouac, *On the Road*, 161). Here again, Kerouac is clearly making reference to finding a destination or a home of some sort where he can rest not only his body, but find a home port where he could rest his restless soul.

As the book progresses, Sal's and Dean's adventures become even more aimless, and Sal begins to question not only his own search, but also the search that his friends are pursuing. About halfway through the book, Sal directly criticizes Dean and the other friends that are accompanying him. As they are driving off after visiting one friend, Paradise says,

> It was sad to see his tall figure receding in the dark as we drove away, just like the other figures in New York and New Orleans: they stand uncertainly underneath immense skies, and everything about them is drowned. Where go? what do? what for?—sleep. But this foolish gang was bending onward. (Kerouac, *On the Road*, 167)

But Sal Paradise does not and cannot tell us onward to where. Sal Paradise realizes in his book that his group of friends is aimlessly roaming around the continent with no set destination in mind. And, unlike at the beginning of the novel when Paradise believes that his group of friends can provide him with answers, he begins to realize that his friends cannot. As the novel progresses, Sal gradually loses faith in Dean and his carefree lifestyle, but he does not lose faith in the road. He decides to resume his own individual search and eventually, Sal Paradise finally and accidently, stumbles over a *satori*, or a moment of sudden enlightenment:

> I walked around, picking butts from the street. I passed a fish'n' chips joint on Market Street, and suddenly the woman in there gave me a terrified look as I passed; she was the proprietress, she apparently thought I was coming in there with a gun to hold up the joint. I walked on a few feet. It suddenly occurred to me this was my mother of about two hundred years ago in England, and that I was her footpad son, returning ... to haunt her honest labors in the hashery. I stopped, frozen with ecstasy on the sidewalk. I looked down Market Street. I didn't know whether it was that or Canal Street in New Orleans: it led to water, ambiguous, universal water, just as 42nd Street in New York, leads to water, and you never know where you are. I thought of Ed Dunkel's ghost on Times Square. I was delirious. I wanted to go back and leer at my strange Dickensian mother in the hash joint. I tingled all over from head to foot. It seemed I had a whole host of memories leading back to 1750 in England and that I was in San Francisco now only in another life and in another body. "No, that woman seemed to say with that terrified glance, "don't come back and plague your honest, hard-working mother ... you are no good, inclined to drunkenness and routs and final disgraceful robbery of the fruits of my 'umble labors in the hashery. O son! did you not ever go on your knees and pray for deliverance for all your sins and scoundrel's acts? Lost boy! Depart! (Kerouac, *On the Road*, 172, 173)

In response to this transcendental (possibly somewhat existential) thought, Kerouac goes on to describe this moment and what it meant to him:

> And for just a moment I had reached the point of ecstasy that I always wanted to reach, which was the complete step across chronological time into timeless shadows, and wonderment in the bleakness of the mortal realm, and the sensation of death kicking at my heels, and myself hurrying to a plank where all the angels dove off and flew into the holy void of uncreated emptiness,

the potent and inconceivable radiances shining in bright Mind Essence, innumerable lotuslands falling open in the bright moth swarm of heaven. (Kerouac, *On the Road*, 173)

In these two excerpts, we can see a Kerouac who apparently has visions of himself in another land and time. This transcendental experience is an important part of the discovery of Kerouac's search, as though serving as some kind of message from God providing some orientation in the decisions he is having to make. Kerouac, through his autobiographical character, Sal Paradise, shows himself happy to have had this vision and believes that it allowed him to break the boundaries of normal time, giving him the descriptive, image-filled realization he comes to.

This passage also reveals Kerouac's descriptive writing style, which he grappled with for many years before finally perfecting it. The writing style of *On the Road* is extremely important in any analysis of the book itself, for the adventures Kerouac relates are significantly magnified by the writing style. Unfortunately, the published version of *On the Road* we now read is quite different from his original version.

When Kerouac exhaustedly finished his 120-foot scroll novel in three weeks of marathon typing in 1950, he never imagined he would, at the request of Malcolm Cowley, his editor at Viking Press, have to revise, edit, cut, and add so many parts of the story. The 1957 version of the book that readers get, although still strongly in the spirit of Kerouac's "spontaneous prose," cannot begin to compare to the first draft. The 120-foot scroll is the one that Kerouac truly wanted to see published—one that he believed was dictated by the Holy Ghost, as Robert Giroux—one of his editors at Viking Press—explains.

However, the published version of *On the Road* still manages to strongly reveal and describe the complexity and intermingling of Kerouac's and Neal Cassady's search. Tragically, what Kerouac apparently concluded from his time spent out on the West coast with Neal Cassady and his other friends was this: "What I accomplished by coming to Frisco I don't know" (Kerouac, *On the Road*, 177). He also has Sal Paradise say a few pages later, "I looked everywhere for the sad and fabled tinsmith of my mind" (Kerouac, *On the Road*, 180). Kerouac, through his autobiographical character, Sal Paradise, vicariously relates his adventures and thoughts to readers, and allows us to share in the process of exploration and discovery with him. After Sal and Dean engage in a heated argument, Paradise concludes that he and Moriarty are on a quest for different things; he accuses Moriarty of being selfish and careless and, about two-thirds of the way through the book, they decide to part ways and travel different roads.

Once on his own, Paradise still constantly thinks about Moriarty and the adventures he must be having, and it is not long before Paradise winds up knocking again on Moriarty's front door. Paradise does so because he believes that Moriarty is enlightened in some way and embodies the essential qualities of freedom. A friend of Dean Moriarty and Sal Paradise named Galatea says to Paradise one day, "Someday Dean's going to go on one of these trips and never come back" (Kerouac, *On the Road*, 205). In addition, and ironically, Paradise has an afterthought: "With frantic Dean I was rushing through the world without a chance to see it" (Kerouac, *On the Road*, 205). Clearly, Sal Paradise is feeling the push and pull of these two extremes: at one end he is waiting to be magically enlightened by Dean Moriarty, yet Moriarty's haphazard, unstructured, reckless, aimless lifestyle contradicts the thoughtfulness and patience Paradise believes to be necessary elements in his own quest for discovery.

As the two renew their "searching" travels across the continent, their trip keeps getting worse. Their car keeps breaking down and both suffer from nausea in the morning. Yet Moriarty continues and at one point says:

> "Sal, we gotta go and never stop going till we get there."
> "Where we going, man?"
> "I don't know but we gotta go." (Kerouac, *On the Road*, 238)

In the conclusion of the book, Moriarty and Paradise split up and again go their own ways. Kerouac begins one of his final chapters of the novel with the following lyrics to a song:

> Home in Missoula,
> Home in Truckee,
> Home in Opelousas,
> Ain't no home for me. Home in old Medora,
> Home in Wounded Knee,
> Home in Ogallala,
> Home I never be. (Kerouac, *On the Road*, 255)

Sal Paradise eventually concludes that he will never really be home, and if we look at Kerouac's own life, we realize that Kerouac and Sal Paradise do indeed have a great deal in common. For Kerouac, it will indeed be years before he, like Sal, feels that he is home again. Sal Paradise's meaning of home not only implies the physical, geographical location of where one lives. More importantly, it is actually a desire to *genuinely feel* an authentic sense that he really has found a home port for his own wandering soul. In *On the Road*, Kerouac initially thinks that his search for epiphany should be turned inward. His spiritually and morally based writing reflects this belief, but it would take Kerouac some time before he stopped searching in the physical world to find that which would ease his inner soul.

At the end of *On the Road*, Dean and Sal head down south into Mexico, and Sal, as narrator, says, "We had finally found the magic land at the end of the road and we never dreamed of the extent of the magic" (Kerouac, *On the Road*, 276). This magic land is Mexico. Dean and Sal are fascinated by the simplicity of the lives that the Mexican people lead, and believe that there is much more freedom there than they ever found on the west coast of America. Dean Moriarty calls Mexico "heaven" because "there's no suspicion here, nothing like that and all its people here are straight and kind and don't put down any bull" to which Sal adds that "the sun rose pure on pure and ancient activities of human life" (Kerouac, *On the Road*, 278).

Yet Dean Moriarty's anxiety and restlessness ultimately leave him equally restless in Mexico, and, he believes that "the road will get more interesting, especially ahead, always ahead" (Kerouac, *On the Road*, 279). Moreover, again, his influence carries Sal Paradise with him. Sal, however, while in Moriarty's company, is still able to find answers for his own questions and have epiphanies of his own. While in Mexico, they decide to rest one night in the middle of a road in a tropical area, and Sal has an epiphany in the humid night, while lying on the hood of the car:

> For the first time in my life the weather was not something that touched me, that caressed me, froze or seated me, but became me. The atmosphere and I became the same. Soft infinitesimal showers of microscopic bugs fanned down on my face as I slept, and they were extremely pleasant and soothing. The sky was starless, utterly unseen and heavy. I could lie there all night long with my face exposed to the heavens, and it would do me no more harm than a velvet drape drawn over me. The dead bugs mingled with my blood; the live mosquitos exchanged further portions; I began to tingle all over and to smell the rank, hot, and rotten

> jungle, all over from hair and face to feet and toes. (Kerouac, *On the Road*, 295)

Here, Kerouac apparently has had and recorded another transcendental epiphany of sorts, one that takes a pantheistic direction. Kerouac, through Sal Paradise, says that the atmosphere and the weather "became him" and even the insects come in "infinitesimal showers"; Paradise seems to establish a sense of oneness with nature, time, and the universe. This excerpt is important because it reveals Sal's individual and independent search for answers and reveals the revelations he had without the help, influence, or aid of Dean Moriarty, who was still merely "looking for the next and highest and final pass" (Kerouac, *On the Road*, 299).

Sal Paradise's idealism about Mexico and its simplicity also is an indirect criticism of the destructive, technological America of which he is a citizen. One can make the argument that he and Dean are somehow similar to the expatriates who fled to Paris in the 1920s. Kerouac follows by having Sal make a criticism of the United States when he compares the people of America to those in Mexico:

> They didn't know that a bomb had come that could crack all our bridges and roads and reduce them to jumbles, and we would be as poor as they someday, and stretching out our hands in the same, same way. (Kerouac, *On the Road*, 299)

In this line we can see that Kerouac, through Sal, is directly criticizing America's creation of the atomic bomb and making the reader aware that Mexico's citizens do not worry about things like this. The Cold War had a profound impact on America's citizens, looming over them at all times, but less so on the Mexican peasantry. Sal's fascination with their simplicity also leads him to mention his own faith and religious convictions. When Sal wakes up one morning, he excitedly tells Dean, "Man, man, wake up and see the shepherds, wake up and see the golden world that Jesus came from, with your own eyes you can tell" (Kerouac, *On the Road*, 300).

Although Sal Paradise never really writes specifically about his own religion, his comments reveal both directly and indirectly his own Christian faith. His reference to Jesus and the "golden world that he came from" reveals Sal Paradise's *and* Jack Kerouac's continuing belief in Christianity—and more specifically, Catholicism.

Kerouac, however, retains as well a mystical, magical attitude in his literature at this time that deals with some supernatural moments or encounters that also serve as epiphanies:

> In the fall I myself started back home from Mexico City and one night just over Laredo border in Dilley, Texas, I was standing on the hot road underneath an arc-lamp with the summer moths smashing into it when I heard the sound of footsteps from the darkness beyond, and lo, a tall old man with flowing white hair came clomping by with the a pack on his back, and when he saw me as he passed, he said, "Go moan for man" and clomped on back to his dark. Did this mean that I should at last go on my pilgrimage on foot on the dark roads around America? I struggled and hurried to New York, and one night I was standing in a dark street in Manhattan and called up to the window of a loft where I thought my friends were having a party. But a pretty girl stuck her head out the window and said "Yes? Who is it?"
>
> "Sal Paradise," I said, and heard my name resound in the sad and empty street.
>
> "Come on up," she called. "I'm making hot chocolate." So I went up and there she was, the girl with the pure and innocent dear eyes that I had always searched for and for so long. We agreed to love each other madly. (Kerouac, *On the Road*, 306)

The mystical stranger that Sal Paradise meets serves as another epiphany. His coming out of the darkness and quickly vanishing into it again, only to tell Paradise to "go moan for man" provides an extremely pessimistic and fatalistic view, not only of mankind, but of life and existence in general. This experience also reinforces the belief of some critics that Jack Kerouac uses the name Sal Paradise to sound like "Sad Paradise," and may be Kerouac's attempt to articulate his world-view. This view seems supported by Kerouac's conclusions in the book, of which the last to be described is:

> So in America when the sun goes down and I sit on the old broken-down river pier watching all that road going, all the people dreaming in the immensity of it, and in Iowa I know by now the children must be crying in the land where they let the children cry ... and nobody, nobody knows what's going to happen to anybody besides the forlorn rags of growing old, I think of Dean Moriarty, I even think of Old Dean Moriarty the father we never found, I think of Dean Moriarty. (Kerouac, *On the Road*, 310)

In this passage, this sense of the world being a "sad paradise" is reinforced by Kerouac's words via Sal Paradise. Sal Paradise for once has decided to sit and watch "all that road going, all the people dreaming in the immensity of it"; to watch people like himself who believe that the adventures of the road do, indeed, hold some secrets. Nevertheless, Paradise also seems to say this as if the road is really just an idealistic image that actually holds no secrets, and that the dreams people have remain just that—dreams. This somewhat despondent conclusion ends with Paradise saying that "nobody, nobody knows what's going to happen to anybody besides the forlorn rags of growing old," and this is all that Sal Paradise can conclude.

The tone of *On the Road* suggests that Sal Paradise discovered that many of his adventures on the road were empty of meaning and the truths that he did find were stumbled upon haphazardly. What Sal Paradise hoped to find was a home, both a physical place to call home and a sense that he had actually found a homeport for his restless soul. The woman he meets back in New York at the end of the novel also helps the reader confirm that Sal Paradise *did* find the love that he was yearning so desperately to find.

In the first draft Kerouac's firsthand experiences were written down using actual names, and what he was telling in the book was simply his own life story. The elements he eventually changed were due to Malcolm Cowley's suggestions and led to the publication of the novel that has now become a modern American literary classic. Kerouac was advised by Cowley, at that time chief editor of Viking Press, to combine several of the trips to reduce repetition and gain clarity. Names were also changed in fear of libel, especially those of characters who use drugs in the book. The style, however, manages to actually retain the spirit of spontaneous prose. Although Kerouac had to do significant editing and revising before the novel was published seven years after it was written, the passionate spirit poured into that original 120-foot roll novel somehow still survived, and it is the energy that still captures the attention of readers today.

This "middle" period of Kerouac's life continued for four more years; he kept searching in the outer world for answers. One discovery that Jack Kerouac did find at this time was his new writing style of spontaneous prose. This kind of writing had for Kerouac a very moral and religious significance; he believed that anything that the mind conceptualized should be written down as purely as possible exactly as thought, and as the brain reacts to it, therefore allowing emotions to flow with the thoughts onto the page.

This new technique, "which has sometimes been called Instant Literature (Wakefield, 70), is explained by Kerouac as:

> a new way of writing about life, no fiction, no craft, no revising afterthoughts, the heartbreaking discipline of the veritable fire ordeal where you can't go back but have made the vow of "speak now or forever hold your tongue" and all of it innocent go ahead confession, the discipline of making the mind the slave of the tongue with no chance to lie or reelaborate ... (Wakefield, 70)

Whatever the drawbacks of that method, it enabled Kerouac to accelerate his literary production at a terrific rate. It had taken him three years to write the traditional *The Town and the City*, but using his new instant formula, he wrote *On the Road* in just *three weeks* and, in a mighty record-breaking burst, raced through *The Subterraneans* in merely *three days and nights*.

Chapter 5

Spontaneous Prose: The Subterraneans, Book of Dreams, and Mexico City Blues

Jack Kerouac wrote *The Subterraneans* shortly after writing *On the Road*, when he had abandoned hope of having any of his material—written in this new style—ever published. However, fortunately for Kerouac, this sense of defeat allowed him to write as he truly wished without any artistic constraints or limitations.

The Subterraneans focuses on Leo Percepied (again, a thinly disguised Jack Kerouac) and the relationship he develops with an African-American woman named Mardou Fox. The book, as did others, reveals a very thoughtful, caring, and overly concerned character that falls in love. Because of a dream Leo experiences one night—that his girlfriend had an affair with one of his friends—he decides to break up with her. He leaves her, goes back home to live with his mother, and writes a book. As before, Jack Kerouac *really* did have this experience, and, as before, when publishing the novel six years later, to avoid libel, he again changed the names of all the characters, including himself.

Kerouac's use of names in his novels is not accidental. In this case, "Leo Percepied" is used to reveal Kerouac's views of himself. Leo was Kerouac's father's name, whose death in 1946 triggered Kerouac's writing of *The Town and the City*. Gerald Nicosia, one of Kerouac's biographers explained Kerouac's theory of how "Percepied" is French for "pierced foot ... Oedipus of the Greek legend had his feet pierced as a child and derived his name from that wound, 'Oedipus' being Greek for swollen foot, the condition caused by his injury. While punning on percipient (or perceptive), one who perceives, Kerouac also identifies Leo with Oedipus on a number of levels" (Nicosia, 449). Nicosia offers the following analysis:

> ... one of Leo's problems is that he replaced his father in his mother's affections, and has in turn accepted her as his "wife"; ...

Excerpts from *Gerald Nicosia, Memory Babe: A Critical Biography of Jack Kerouac*. Copyright © 1994 by University of California Press. Reprinted with permission.

His affair with Mardou takes on significance in light of Kerouac's new interest in Reich, since Reich believed the Oedipal complex could be rendered harmless once one's damned-up sexual energy found a normal outlet.

Metaphysically, Leo and Oedipus suffer the same dilemma. Told by the Delphic Oracle that he will kill his father and marry his mother, Oedipus moves to another city to frustrate the prophecy, thereby facilitating its fulfillment. Seeking to evade his prophetic dream of losing Mardou, Leo precipitates the event. At the end of *Oedipus Rex*, horrified to realize that "those calamities we inflict on ourselves are those which cause the most pain," Oedipus stabs out his eyes. At the end of *The Subterraneans*, Leo merely goes on to new visions—of his mother's loving face, and of Yuri as a "Funny Angel." (Nicosia, 449)

Yuri is the fictional name of one of Kerouac's real friends who develops a strong interest in Mardou. One day, after Leo Percepied tells Mardou about his dream, she tells him to ignore it for it was only a dream, but at this time in Kerouac's personal life, he was exploring the "dreamlike nature of reality, and the reality of dreams" (Nicosia, 448). Kerouac's anguish to somehow actually make this dream a reality results in a self-fulfilling prophecy. But the breakup is his own fault because in the novel, Leo is constantly telling, explaining, and reminding Mardou about this particular dream. By the end of the novel, Mardou's interest in Yuri does, indeed, develop, but only after Leo had so forcefully planted the idea in her head. Mardou decides that as an independent woman she will do what she wants and concludes that Leo brought it upon himself.

This novel reveals the quintessential style of Kerouac and, fortunately for both reader and writer, the novel was published as originally written, or, at least, much more closely than was *On the Road*. It seems that in *The Subterraneans*, plot and style overlap fully. Jack Kerouac as a novelist was trying to discover and improve his writing method, which helped him reach deeper understandings of his material. Leo Percepied, Kerouac's persona, was on a quest for love and, more importantly, an *understanding* of love:

... the power of *The Subterraneans* derives from Kerouac finally having a literary theory that complemented his own incapacity to live as detachedly as he wanted to write .... Kerouac saw the critical and academic restrictions on prose form as ruinous to both the writer and his work. The very essence of this new literary method was engagement, concern for the material written about, and a coming together of mind and subject. To Ed White (a literary friend), Kerouac explained that he was trying "to swirl my brain from common-place expression into seas of English ..." He declared his belief that "no writing mattered unless it contained this ... intensity" ... to blow (like Jazz musicians), to use bop phrases excitedly beyond stringencies of sentences. ... The next step in English literature, he believed, would come from "the bio electric flow ... from the center of the mind and jewel point of interest in memory or vision therein outward ... like one wild impulse surge electric language ..."

In his estimation, rules and punctuation were secondary to sounds, rhythms, and the "electric fury" of the writer himself, who should ideally be in tune with the electro-magnetic "cosmic energy" postulated by both Einstein and Reich. As an example, Jack instructed Ed not to write about the history of the Denver City Council but rather to "start writing about that fascinating little red bud on the bleak bush in front of the City and County Building or something you understand or bums ... or jewel of personal colloquial interest. ..." (Nicosia, 446, 447)

In this passage, many important statements should be noted. Kerouac at this time had almost perfected his spontaneous prose style. His well-defined theory on the effects this style of writing would have for both reader and writer show him to be reflective and devoted to his craft. Kerouac was tired of working with "academic restrictions on prose form" (Clark); he had worked with these in his writing of the *The Town and the City*, which he himself dismissed as a "novel novel" (Clark) because of its traditional, predictable, imitative, and derivative format. His interest in jazz music also appears, and he believes that the writer, like the musician should "blow" (Clark) all the music, or all the words, everything from within one's soul.

The *Subterraneans* can be seen as an "organic whole" in that Percepied feels guilty in the novel for not being able to support Mardou and confesses his soul to her, telling her everything he feels about their relationship. The language Kerouac has Percepied use promotes these revelations, hiding nothing and confessing all.

In this novel, too, Leo Percepied is trying to make sense of his relationship and the way his attention shifted from his mother to Mardou Fox, the female character in Kerouac's story. He feels guilt over that kind of shift in his real life because Kerouac and his mother were extremely close. Leo feels guilt that he does not have the money to support Mardou, and, instead, Mardou is supporting him. To add to these problems, Percepied is trying to come to terms with his dream of Mardou's affair with Yuri. Percepied, like Kerouac, believes that everything and every aspect of life is intertwined, and every facet of life, in turn, becomes the factor and cause of another event. With this view, Percepied's dream obviously has significance, or else, he believes, he never would have had it. Mardou tries convincing Leo that dreams are of no significance, but Leo is convinced otherwise, and it is his tenacious belief in the validity of the dream that ends up ruining their relationship.

Kerouac wrote this novel in three days in the fall of 1953 directly after his love affair with Mardou ended, and "the final verdict rendered by the book is that for Kerouac, love and his art could not coexist" (Dardess, 295). *The Subterraneans* not only describes the ending of a love affair, but the work itself is the very cause of that ending. Kerouac's writing at this time became an "act of worship," and Kerouac knew that at least for him, art and love could not coexist; eventually, one would win over the other:

> Kerouac's bedrooms within the various apartments and houses he shared with his mother were frequently described by visitors as looking like a monk's cell: sparse, meticulously neat, with a crucifix over the bed, a box or file for manuscripts and correspondence, a typewriter on a table, and a chair. Spontaneous prose required this austerity if the confession were to be purified. Kerouac nowhere says that spontaneous prose required an identical austerity from all confessors, but it did so from him. And no one regretted what was thereby lost more than he did. (Dardess, 296)

The Subterraneans shows Kerouac's ongoing quest for love and for the soul-searching woman he hoped to find who would somehow bring a sense of tranquility to his life. Equally important, the novel also shows Kerouac's ongoing efforts to develop and hone a writing style that would allow total confession—total release of thoughts and feelings trapped inside waiting to explode and transcribed onto paper. This book is quintessential Kerouac not only in its style, but also in that in it, again, Kerouac has to make a life decision on whether he actually wants to develop a relationship with a woman or choose a life of emotionally painful and laborious writing. He chooses writing, and his decision leads to his most experimental literary period.

By early 1954 Kerouac's "complexity of attitude was a direct result of his extreme sensitivity to the fallen beauty of life" (Clark); he had convinced himself that publishers would never again take a chance on his novels. Years before, Kerouac had submitted *On the Road* to several publishing companies in its original version and had been rejected many times. Although Viking showed an interest, it was not strong enough to make them optimistic in it, so, starting in 1951, Kerouac decided to write only for himself. As noted, *The Subterraneans* was the first book in which Kerouac felt like he was allowed to explore and experiment freely with his style, and the books that followed show a continuing courageousness to experiment with both style and subject matter.

The role that dreams played in Kerouac's life was something that Kerouac examined still further after his breakup with the woman who became "Mardou Fox." What resulted was his book written in April of 1954 he titled *Book of Dreams*. This book was simply "a journal of his actual dreams, recorded hastily as soon as he awakened in order to capture the bemused and mystified logic of dreams in equally hazy fragmentary prose" (Nicosia, 463).

The Foreword and the Preface of the book, also written by Kerouac, give readers a valuable insight as to what he hoped to accomplish:

> The reader should know that this is just a collection of dreams that I scribbled after I woke up from my sleep—They were all written spontaneously, nonstop, just like dreams happen, sometimes written before I was even wide awake—The characters that I've written about in my novels reappear in these dreams in weird new situations and they continue the same story which is the one story that I always write about. ... And good because the fact that everybody in the world dreams every night ties all mankind together shall we say in one unspoken Union and also proves that the world is really transcendental which the Communists do not believe because they think their dreams are 'unrealities' instead of visions of what they saw in their sleep.
> So I dedicate this book of dreams to the roses of the unborn. (Kerouac, *Book of Dreams*, 1)

On the next page, Jack Kerouac writes in the Preface:

> *Book of Dreams* was the easiest book to write—When I woke up from my sleep I just lay there looking at the pictures that were

Excerpts from Jack Kerouac, *Book of Dreams*. Copyright © 2001 by City Lights.

> fading slowly like in a movie fadeout into the recesses of my sub-
> conscious mind—As soon (one minute or so) as I had assembled
> them together with any earlier dreams of the evening I could
> catch, like fish in a deep pool, I got my weary bones out of bed
> & through eyes swollen with sleep swiftly scribbled in pencil in
> my little dream notebook till I had exhausted every rememberable
> item—I wrote nonstop so that the subconscious could speak for
> itself in its own form, that is, uninterruptedly flowing & rippling—
> Being half awake I hardly knew what I was doing let alone writing.
> … Everybody interested in their dreams should use the method
> of fishing their dreams out in time before they disappear forever.
> (Kerouac, *Book of Dreams*, 3, 4)

Here, Kerouac is using his spontaneous prose style to explain the reasons and methods used to record his dreams. By this time, Kerouac had already largely perfected his style, but he was still on a personal search for the meaning that dreams play in our daily lives, and the text is valuable for that reason. Kerouac was developing and reinforcing the faith he had in dreams. He also mentions that this book is really a continuation of the same story he always writes. This idea is important because Kerouac's life, as he views and interprets it, is really a fragmented but developing continuous whole. His belief that dreams tie all of humanity together in one "unspoken Union" gives insight into Kerouac's worldview at this time.

Again, Kerouac's writing technique here incorporates the use of spontaneous prose at an even deeper level, in that Kerouac says he is half-asleep and only half-conscious as he writes, unequivocally placing his faith in his subconscious mind. Kerouac believed that dreams are important and should be examined by everyone before "they disappear forever." The book—or notebook—is almost two hundred pages long, and dream follows dream. Kerouac uses his spontaneous prose style in describing everything and everyone, and the dreams provide not only a "substrata" (Ferlinghetti) for his other novels, but a "substrata" about his life which somehow "string all of his nights together" (Ferlinghetti).

One of Kerouac's particular dreams serves as a representative of the others:

> In a strange living room presumably in Mexico City but very much
> and suspiciously like a livingroom in a dream of my Ma and Pa in
> Lowell or Dream Movetown—June (Evans) is telling me the name
> of a great unknown Greek writer, Plipias, Snipias, how his father

> ran away with the family money so Plipias, queer, went to live
> on an Island with the boy he loves; and wrote: "I never go on
> strike against man, because I love him"—June recommended this
> writer highly, and said: "You spend an hour a day hassling over
> small things but in the larger sense you can see what he means,
> never go on strike against man." Meanwhile, I'm about to go in
> the bathroom but Bull's already in there—has made no comment.
> (Kerouac, *Book of Dreams*, 9)

This dream is representative of many others, and what is significant is that Kerouac mentions many of his experiences but blurs them together. For example, he mentions Mexico City, where he had visited frequently and lived for several months; he also mentions his mother and father in his boyhood hometown of Lowell, possibly indicating the ongoing influence of his parents on his life. He also mentions a Greek writer, though uncertain of the name, which shows the firm grasp of literature on his own life. Literature and reality were thoroughly intermixed for Kerouac. Finally, he mentions a bit of philosophy in the message that he is given to "Never go on strike against man"; this message reveals Kerouac's love of life and the value he placed on humanity. Additionally and importantly, it reveals his habitual reflectiveness.

Fictional characters from his two previous novels also reappear in his dreams, along with individuals who were an important part of Kerouac's life. Kerouac sometimes makes references to other writers, and everything in his dreams seems inextricably intertwined: reality, fiction, literature, as well as family all find a common ground in unification in his dreams. He even makes many half-conscious philosophical statements about life in general in some of his dreams, such as:

> ... As I say, words, images & dreams are fingers of false imagination
> pointing at the reality of Holy Emptiness—but my words are still
> many & my images stretch to the holy void like a road that has an
> end—It's the ROAD OF THE HOLY VOID this writing, this life, this
> image of regrets. (Kerouac, *Book of Dreams*, 157)

Book of Dreams is a journey into Kerouac's deepest, innermost subconscious thoughts. Moreover, the way he expresses his dreams and what he chooses to explain in further detail give the reader an insight into the intermixture that was Kerouac's life, where reality, fiction, and literature were all inextricably intertwined as he attempted to form one coherent, organic whole.

An essential factor to mention is that by 1954, Kerouac was already looking for a new "source of harmony" and he found it after reading Ashvaghosha's
Life of Buddha. Allen Ginsberg's study of Eastern religions and Kerouac's
meeting Gary Snyder were instrumental in providing Kerouac with both the
principal and secondary information that Kerouac began delving into in his
studies of Buddhism. He also read Henry David Thoreau's *Walden, or Life in
the Woods* and took a stronger interest in nature and meditation as a result.
For the next few years, he

> ... absorbed himself in literature and practice first and primarily
> of Mahayana and then of Zen Buddhism, and this absorption is
> apparent in the large volume of writing that dates from this period.
> The years between 1954 and 1957 were perhaps Kerouac's most
> fruitful. Assessing the fruitfulness is made difficult by the fact that
> most of Kerouac's explicitly Buddhist writings have never been
> published. "Some of the Dharma," a large book of Buddhist prayers;
> 'Buddha Tells Us', Kerouac's version of the *Surangama Sutra*; and
> "Wake Up," a biography of the Buddha, are still in manuscript. But
> in (some of his published) books, Buddhism plays a subordinate,
> though powerful role. It assumes a place within what seemed to
> him the larger structure of his Roman Catholicism. (Dardess, 296)

Some of the books that reveal the influence of Buddhism on his life in-
clude *Mexico City Blues*, which is a work containing extremely experimental
poetry, *The Scripture of the Golden Eternity*, *Visions of Gerard*, *The Dharma
Bums*, *Desolation Angels*, and *Satori in Paris*. Late in this middle period of
his writing, Kerouac was becoming acquainted, specifically, with Zen
Buddhism, and although his work begins to show a shift in literary style
and content when compared to *The Town and the City* and *On the Road*, his
epiphanies have not yet reached the more mature stage that reveal poignant
insight and wisdom, as they finally do in Kerouac's late literary period.

Kerouac's attraction to Buddhism came because it resolved the:

> ... paradox that tore him apart of God's seemingly simultaneous
> presence and absence in the world he saw and Kerouac could
> seize with relief on Buddhism's annihilation of the paradox. The
> suffering of all created things under a sky emptied of divinity could
> never be ignored, but it could be tolerated and even accepted if
> it were viewed, not as a sign of sin, but as an illusion from which
> Buddhists might release themselves through the careful practice
> of ritual. (Dardess, 296)

Kerouac was instantly captivated by Buddhism and its teachings that "each man must find his own path to final peace and knowledge through his own efforts" and to "look within, thou art Buddha" (Ross, 80). His writings in *Mexico City Blues* reflect these meditations, and Kerouac was further attracted to Buddhism by its precept that "consciousness was attained only spontaneously, since the conventional categories of thought were themselves symptoms of the illusion from which one sought to be freed" (Dardess, 296). This commitment to spontaneity of consciousness leads to Kerouac's sometimes playful language in some of the poetry; it also explains and helps to justify his sincere attempt to figure out some of the mysteries of life. *Book of Dreams* is noticeably pivotal because in it, Kerouac explores the world of thought, the world of himself, and the world around him, without doing any actual traveling across America or into Mexico. Kerouac is now writing and creating poetry—no longer triggered by physical and autobiographical incidents or adventures—as he had done in his three previous books.

Many of these poems, or choruses, were, indeed, written in the spirit of spontaneity, but Kerouac wrote many of them not with the speed that had seemed so essential in his previous writings, but rather with a *controlled* spontaneity, in that many "were written at the carefully measured rate of one line per hour" (Nicosia, 480). Kerouac would sit down with a "cup of coffee … on his tiny rooftop for a few hours every morning, penciling little blues poems in his notebooks" (Nicosia, 480). His specific innovation was in freeing himself from all other artificial measure and, as Allen Ginsberg says, "Going out into the mind itself to find the shape of the poem" (Nicosia, 481).

Some of the statements that Kerouac makes in *Mexico City Blues* are remarkably different from what he writes in his first books, and they clearly show the growing influence of Buddhism on his life. For example, in the 169th Chorus—Choruses having no titles, being numbered only—Kerouac writes:

> Lie down
> Rest
> Breathe slowly
> Dead in Time
> You're dead already
> What's a little bit more time got to do with it
> So you're dead
> So the living Loathe the Dead, themselves
> So forgive, reassure, pat, protect,
> and purify them

Excerpts from Jack Kerouac, *Mexico City Blues*. Copyright © 1990 by Grove Atlantic, Inc.

Whatever way is best.
Thus Spake, Tathagata ...
Dead in Time—Rest in Time. (Kerouac, *Mexico City Blues*, 169)

The first three lines of the poem directly contradict the themes seen in Kerouac's early writings and amply reveal the strong Buddhist influence on Kerouac. Kerouac now presents a radically new vision of life and existence, and a positive one at that, in that Kerouac says, "So forgive, reassure, pat, protect, and purify them whatever way is best." Although we may be "dead in time," Kerouac believes that we should not worry much about it, but "rest in time"—rest which might be understood to mean tranquility and optimism.

In the 190th Chorus, Kerouac writes:

What have I attained in Buddhism is nothing.
What I wish to attain,
is nothing.
Let me explain.
In perceiving the Dharma I
achieved nothing. What worries me is not nothing
But everything, the trouble is number,
But since everything is nothing
then I am worried nil.
In seeking to attain the Dharma
I failed, attaining nothing,
And so I succeeded the goal,
Which was, pure happy nothing.
No matter how you cut it
It's empty delightful boloney. (Kerouac, *Mexico City Blues*, 190)

In this chorus, Kerouac describes the void, or the idea that life exists in the concept and understanding of the idea of everything (ness) and nothingness, coexisting as innate counterparts of each other. Kerouac never complains, though, about the fact that he has found nothing in Buddhism because he ultimately wishes to attain nothing anyway. He seems to be content with his belief in the "pure happy nothing" because to him, life is really a temporary experience that must end with physical death someday. Kerouac comes to realize that although life is temporary, it still has the possibility for great moments of achievement, discovery, and joy. Concerning Kerouac's style,

... though his sentences acquired by cadences and terminologies of the sutras he had been studying, they never lost their other points of reference, the ones that identified Kerouac as a member of the suffering creation, the illusion of whose existence he was supposedly learning to free himself from. (Dardess, 296)

Mexico City Blues "roams widely across continents and cultures in a restless search for meaning and expression, giving the verse the unique qualities found in America's most distinctive contribution to music," as described by Kerouac's publisher, Grove Weidenfeld. Despite the fact the book was written in September of 1955, it was not published until 1959. By the time the book was published, Kerouac had become a literary celebrity and cultural hero, and it is interesting to note that he "consistently autographed copies of the book by placing a cross under his signature, a practice he didn't normally use for his other books" (Nicosia, 490). Although Jack Kerouac never really lost or abandoned his Catholic faith, his interest in and solace from Buddhism continued to permeate his literary productions in the period between 1955 and 1958.

Book of Dreams and *Mexico City Blues* mark the transition into Kerouac's final literary period of his life, which can be described as an ongoing, dynamic, and active search into his own mind and soul. This late period shows deliberateness and sobriety in his writings and thoughts, and the epiphanies he reaches during this period are mature and amply reveal deep insight and wisdom. Kerouac now turns his search for epiphany inward and begins examining his inner life with the same curiosity, tenacity, and energy he had when he was searching for answers in the outer world.

Chapter 6

Visions of Gerard *and* The Scripture of the Golden Eternity

J ack Kerouac began writing *Visions of Gerard* in late December of 1955 and finished the manuscript on January 16, 1956, just a few months after *Mexico City Blues*. Kerouac's Buddhist influence is apparent in *Visions of Gerard* by the simple fact that in it, Kerouac is actually taking time out to sit down and analyze how his brother's death in 1926 emotionally affected him and this influence is revealed in the conclusions he reaches. He is no longer looking to the outer world, nor is he influenced by his friends; these preoccupations no longer serve as the basis of his books. Kerouac now begins looking exclusively at his individual life and begins to delve into his own soul and mind, and the conclusions he reaches in his books reveal a mature writer and an individual who is attempting to grow spiritually. Many biographers of Kerouac see in this book a definite shift in his literature:

> Once written, *Visions of Gerard* becomes the cornerstone of "The Duluoz Legend," asserting once and for all that the coherence of those novels lies in vision rather than plot, characters, theme, or even, as in Proust, style. After finishing *Visions of Gerard*, Kerouac contemplated adding the word vision to the titles of most of his other novels, changing *Maggie Cassidy* to "Visions of Mary," *October in the Railroad Earth* to "Visions of the Railroad," etc. "The Thread of the Legend" is the sequence of cosmic moments, which depend on a focus from within (the imaginative power) and from without (the reflections of the material universe). *Visions of Gerard* records the birth of such a double vision in the author while exposing its mechanism again and again in the text. The existence of that vision, so established, forces a new reading of all of the writer's other works; in a very real sense it doubles his literary output. (Nicosia, 502)

In *Visions of Gerard* Kerouac writes directly about his older brother who passed away at age nine—when Jack was only five. Now, Jack Kerouac was thirty-two years old. The book reveals the profound impact his brother's death had on his life. Again, Kerouac's interest and studies in Buddhism were making him examine not only the issue of life and death in general, but also making him deeply reflect on his loved ones who had passed, specifically his brother Gerard.

Kerouac is extremely faithful in his effort to write a factual autobiography and gives readers actual names, places, and dates. He writes early in the book:

> ... for the first four years of my life, while he lived, I was Gerard, the world was his face, the flower of his face, the pale stooped disposition, the heartbreakingness and the holiness and his teachings of tenderness to me, and my mother constantly reminding me to pay attention to his goodness and advice for me the first four years of my life are permeant and gray with the memory of a kindly serious face bending over me and being me and blessing me. ... (Kerouac, *Visions of Gerard*, 2)

With this novel, Kerouac seems to arrive at a gradual understanding of Gerard's purpose in life and a gradual understanding of death in general. Kerouac continuously makes the claim that he, himself, was Gerard. Extremely pivotal in this book is that Kerouac "traces the lineage of his writing unequivocally to his brother: 'the whole reason why I ever wrote at all ... because of Gerard ... the idealism, Gerard the religious hero—'" (Nicosia, 502). Kerouac confesses that the depth of his writing comes from, and is due to, the loss of Gerard (Nicosia, 503).

In this novel, Gerard's religious message is similar to the introduction in Kerouac's *Mexico City Blues*, which is that "We're all in heaven—but we don't know it" (Nicosia, 502). Nevertheless, Kerouac also begins to negotiate his own religious beliefs, and, as a result, a convoluted mixture of Buddhism and Catholicism appear in the book. Kerouac writes:

> It was only many years later when I met and understood Savas Savakis that I recalled the definite and immortal idealism which had been imparted me by my holy brother—And even later with the discovery (or dullmouthed amazed hang-middled mindburnt waking rediscovery) of Buddhism, Awakenedhood—Amazed recollection that from the very beginning I, whoever 'I' or whatever 'I' was, was destined, destined indeed, to meet, learn, understand

> Gerard and Savas and the Blessed Lord Buddha (and my Sweet
> Christ too through all his Paulian tangles and bloody crosses of
> heathen violence)—To awaken to pure faith in the bright one truth:
> all is well, practice Kindness, Heaven is nigh. (Kerouac, *Visions of
> Gerard*, 6)

Here, Kerouac mixes many elements that result in the formation of one large, coherent view on life. Kerouac describes how he believes *everything* is planned out in life in the shape of destiny, and he affirms his mixed beliefs in his brother's saintliness and the effects Gerard had on his own life, along with his beliefs in "the Blessed Lord Buddha" and "my Sweet Christ too" and that all these beliefs together formed his one bright truth that "All is Well, practice Kindness, Heaven is Nigh." Kerouac never clarifies whether this Heaven is a Catholic Heaven or a Buddhist Heaven, but his blending of religions shows that apparently Kerouac thought it was all *one* Heaven.

The book not only leads significantly to Kerouac's personal growth, but it also leads to a more unified vision of the world that is expressed in his writings. Kerouac's vision of both the world and the craft of writing were becoming more deeply intertwined. This fusion is extremely important because Kerouac's recognition and awareness of this idea of oneness led to writings that significantly and powerfully incorporate autobiography and help to further develop and deepen his ever-expanding and ever-changing worldview. Kerouac was now writing with renewed and greater confidence and had fewer artistic inhibitions.

In *Visions of Gerard*, Kerouac presents his brother as a Buddha figure, and although Gerard was only nine at the time of his death, Kerouac extols his brother's understanding of life and death. What Kerouac concludes is that "It is not that life and death are the same, but rather that one is no truer than another, no more than the image in one's left eye is truer than the image in one's right eye. The two eyes neither confirm nor disprove each other, but their unified sight yields a valuable perspective" (Rpt. in Nicosia, 503).

Kerouac's "visions" of Gerard encourage and allow him to closely examine the relationship between life and death, as well as the relationship between mortality and immortality. Kerouac concludes that like the seasons of a year, life and death are the seasons of life. Though no one season is more important than any other, each plays a complementary role in the cycle of nature. Kerouac concludes that death is an important and essential part of life, and that in these "visions" lie man's salvation, "for what is flawed can always be exhausted, taken out of bounds, overtopped" (Nicosia, 508).

This novel is an affirmation of Kerouac's inner search, and his attempts to comprehend mortality and immortality show a growing religious interest that would develop even further and with much greater complexity in his next book.

The Scripture of the Golden Eternity is the only prose work by Jack Kerouac that does not follow the spontaneous prose method, but it too, shows his struggle to make some kind of sense of this world and find some validity in existence for himself and all of humanity. His personal, religious treatise shows both the influence of Buddhism and Catholicism in his life. Eric Mottram at King's College at The University of London wrote the following about Kerouac and *The Scripture of the Golden Eternity:*

> To achieve personal peace in active joy in this century perhaps more than any other has meant dropping out of the current power structure. Since the second World War for many men (and women) this has meant finding a viable alternative to the drag-ging decay of Christian capitalist democracy and the delusions of extreme leftist reform associated with the Depression and the Thirties. In the Forties and Fifties this alternative consisted in forms of ideological refusal to be held captive by the history of the West. *The Scripture of the Golden Eternity* is Jack Kerouac's statement of confidence in his oneness with the universe of energy and form, a confidence to which his whole being swelled. (Mottram, vii, viii)

At this time, Kerouac was strongly influenced and fascinated by Gary Snyder, a lumberjack-looking poet. Gary Snyder, a fundamental, very well-learned, and very well-read Buddhist, thought that Jack was a "Bodhi Sattva," an enlightened individual who understands the mysteries and se-crets of life, Buddhism, and his own being. It was at his request that Jack wrote *The Scripture of the Golden Eternity.* Jack Kerouac wrote "In pencil, carefully revised and everything, because it was a scripture. I had no right to be spontaneous" (Kerouac, *The Scripture of the Golden Eternity,* X).

For the first time since *The Town and the City,* Kerouac revises and carefully edits his writings. The influence that Buddhism had on Kerouac affected not only his personal life, but his style of writing as well. The same author who had written madly and with furious speed years before without

Excerpts from Jack Kerouac, *The Scripture of the Golden Eternity.* Copyright © 2001 by City Lights.

revising any sentences was now, not only writing deliberately, but was also living deliberately, and *The Scripture of the Golden Eternity* provides insight into his thoughts concerning creation, wisdom, existence, and his sense of oneness with the universe.

Since the *Scripture* appeared in 1960,

> ... ways of living through a traditional sense of oneness with all energy and form have become a common basis for survival in a disastrous time for the intelligent young in America. It is a part of the legacy of the Beat Generation, and part of a constant recall to the value of poetry. In the ... words of Gary Snyder's "Notes on Poetry as an Ecological Survival Technique": poetry can be "the skilled and inspired use of the voice and language to embody rare and powerful states of mind that are in immediate origin personal to the singer, but at deep levels common to all who listen." (Mottram, *The Scripture of the Golden Eternity*, XIII)

The book is also pivotal and reflective of Kerouac's late period, in that Kerouac attempts to set down his beliefs carefully and, therefore, reaches a point of epiphany that he can consciously hold onto. Unlike his early works, in which he hopes to stumble across moments of sudden enlightenment, the discipline in writing *The Scripture of the Golden Eternity* "Kerouac could use to secure himself within that ecstatic love which continually slipped from his grasp by the sheer contingency of day to day living" (Mottram, *The Scripture of the Golden Eternity*, XIV).

The sixty-six piece treatise incorporates tenets of Buddhism, Catholicism, American Native-American Indian beliefs, visions, and dreams, and the result is a deliberate, mature, sober, complex personal vision of the world which concludes that "a joyful modesty [is needed] as the condition of living in the universe without a restless urge to conquest, moral dogmatism and hierarchy" (Mottram, *The Scripture of the Golden Eternity*, XV).

Kerouac now validates his existence with his ability to conceptualize ideas, and his writing style is just as deliberate as his thoughts; Kerouac here merges both thoughts and words with style. Scripture Number One begins with Kerouac stating:

> Did I create that sky? Yes, for if it was anything other than a conception in my mind I wouldn't have said "Sky"—That is why I am the golden eternity. There are not two of us here,

reader and writer, but one, one golden eternity, One-Which-It-Is, That-Which-Everything-Is.

Kerouac is aware that *he* created the concept of the sky for himself, so, therefore, his own concept of sky is the only concept he knows, and consequently, has validity. Kerouac also develops his idea of oneness with the universe in this work; the "golden eternity" not only shows oneness with the universe, but his use of "golden" has a decidedly positive connotation. Kerouac's explanation that he and the reader are really one being shows an emergence of a Buddhist-kind of transcendence. He goes on to say in one of the following scriptures:

> 5. I am the golden eternity in mortal animate form.
> 6. Strictly speaking, there is no me, because all is emptiness. I am empty, I am non-existent. All is bliss.
> 7. This truth law has no more reality than the world.
> 8. You are the golden eternity because there is no me and no you, only one golden eternity.

These examples illustrate Kerouac's sense of oneness with the universe and reveal his acceptance and realization that life and death are equal parts of one eternity. In these scriptures, Kerouac is attempting to unravel the mysteries of life, and what he concludes is that the "truth law" and "the world" equally exist because there really is "no me and no you, only one golden eternity" (Kerouac, *The Scripture of the Golden Eternity*). He seems to peacefully accept his mortality because it is a part of the "golden eternity"; the role that he plays in this world is significant, yet, simultaneously and paradoxically, insignificant as well.

In Scripture Ten he writes:

> 10. This world is a movie of what everything is, it is one movie, made of the same stuff throughout, belonging to nobody, which is what everything is.

Kerouac continues his treatise in this way, making contradictions about the oneness, yet simultaneous sense of nothingness in life. Kerouac's "everything" literally means everything on this earth, all its events, occurrences, cycles, seasons, people, and "the knowledge that sees the golden eternity in all things" (Scripture 13). Kerouac continues by stating this "golden eternity is not even discussable, groupable into words; it is not even endless, in fact, it is not even mysterious or inscrutably inexplicable; it is what is; it is that; it is this. We could easily call the golden eternity "This". But 'what's in a name?' asked Shakespeare" (Scripture 14). In Scripture 45 Kerouac writes:

> When you've understood this scripture, throw it away. If you can't understand this scripture, throw it away. I insist on your freedom.

This passage illustrates Kerouac's ideas concerning the idea of nothingness in life and the Buddhist belief that one should discover the "light" within the self. Kerouac now came to believe that literature could not really teach truth—all it could do was point out some kind of way, or show some kind of path. After reading Kerouac's sixty-six truths, Gary Snyder pointed out that the work "displays Kerouac's fundamental belief in God" (Nicosia, 516).

Kerouac's epiphanies here can be described as "beating lights" going on and off; when the lights are on, a person has a "timeless moment that can be described as consciousness filled to the point of such abundance that the saturation blocks out and blacks out consciousness" (Kerouac). The result is the sixty-six truths that are inextricably linked to one another. Kerouac defines enlightenment as living "in time and in timelessness" (Nicosia, 516). When Kerouac first showed this work to a friend named Locke McCorkle, Jack prefaced it by saying, "While I was writing this, I thought I knew what it meant, but now I don't know anymore" (Nicosia, 517).

Kerouac concludes the work by stating in the last two scriptures:

> 65. This is the first teaching from the golden eternity.
> 66. The second teaching from the golden eternity is that there never was a first teaching from the golden eternity. So be sure.

These last two scriptures contradict themselves and seem to invalidate everything that Kerouac has ordered the reader to do, but the end result is that Kerouac *did find* validation in some of his own thoughts and spirituality, and these scriptures did allow him to grow as an individual, which further allowed him to grow as a writer. Kerouac writes in Scripture 64 that the

> ... 'golden' came from the sun in my eyelids, and the 'eternity' from my sudden instant realization as I woke up that I had just been where it all came from and where it was all returning, the everlasting So, and so never coming or going.

Kerouac's sutra is a controlled "praise for the overwhelming sense of release afforded by contemplation of the 'Dharma Law' which says: 'All things are made of the same thing which is nothing'" (*The Scripture of the Golden Eternity*, XII). Kerouac would begin examining this law even further in his next two books, *Desolation Angels* and *The Dharma Bums*.

Chapter 7

*D*esolation Angels is written in the spirit of spontaneous prose, but seems to be filtered somehow through the discipline that he showed in *The Scripture of the Golden Eternity*. The first half of the book was written while Kerouac spent sixty days on a Mountaintop—Desolation Peak—in the Cascades, by himself as a fire lookout; the second half of the book was written after his sudden emergence into fame with the publication of *On the Road* in 1957. The book continues Kerouac's "turning of every stone of experience" and presents what may be likened to diary entries, although not dated, only simply divided by chronological numbers. In many ways, the book resembles Walt Whitman's *Specimen Days* (1882) a book we know Kerouac read and mentioned often on television interviews.

In *Desolation Angels* the "narrator seeks to pinpoint the occurrence of moments on a cosmic grid, and he isolates them at the places where his life changed direction for it is by the intersection of such vectors that we are able to get our bearings and sensibly steer our path" (Nicosia, 624). The first two parts of the book are titled "Desolation in Solitude" and "Desolation in the World." Again, Kerouac "intimates that the truth is simply a little farther on down the road," although he had previously concluded that the search for truth is hopeless if one does not take time to examine one's spiritual state. *Desolation Angels* is "distinguished by sympathy for its subjects unique in an era of detached, dry-hearted, professional observers" (Nicosia, 624).

Dan Wakefield, a freelance writer who spent the 1963–1964 academic year as a Nieman Fellow at Harvard, wrote an article for *The Atlantic* in July of 1965 titled "Jack Kerouac Comes Home." In that article he praises Kerouac's writings, efforts, and ability and says something that is quite incisive: "Scratch the surface of Kerouac's prose and you are likely to find the heart of Carl Sandburg rather than Celine" (Wakefield, 71). This is particularly important in that Carl Sandburg is considered "the poet of the people" noted for his optimism in humanity and his celebration of the simple, work-ing class—themes that tie all of his works together. Kerouac and Sandburg do indeed have a great deal of overlap and likeness in their hearts and this idea is worthy of later study.

In *Desolation Angels*, Kerouac again explores the meaning of life within what he believes to coexist: the idea and concept of the void of existence. While spending his time alone on Desolation Peak, he made some pivotal discoveries about his life and his relationships with the world around him. In the first pages of the novel, Kerouac begins with a denial of the idea of noth-ingness he had argued for in *The Scripture of the Golden Eternity* by writing: "It's me that's changed and done all this and come and gone and complained and hurt and joyed and yelled, not the Void" (Kerouac, *Desolation Angels*, 3). Kerouac, once again, reveals his Buddhist influence on his adventures. He writes:

> ... Hold together, Jack, pass through everything, and everything is one dream, one appearance, one flash, one sad eye, one crys-tal lucid mystery, one word—Hold still, man, regain your love of life and go down from this mountain and simply be—be—be the infinite fertilities of the one mind of infinity, make no comments, complaints, criticisms, appraisals, avowals, sayings, shooting stars of thought, just flow, flow, be you all, be you what it is, it is only what it always is—Hope is a word like a snow-drift—This is the Great Knowing, this is the Awakening, this is Voidness—So shut up, live, travel, adventure, bless and don't be sorry—(Kerouac, *Desolation Angels*, 5)

Kerouac's complex worldview would remain with him into the final years of his life. Kerouac concludes that he should just "be" and "flow", but he also seems to have developed a new awareness and attitude of kindness for *all* liv-ing things, and this is what Dan Wakefield means by "Kerouac's heart being sympathetic." Kerouac still believes, though, that "the world is a babe's dream and the ecstasy of the golden eternity is all we're going back to" (Kerouac, *Desolation Angels*, 28). However, his restless spirit also surfaces in the text and Kerouac writes:

> I sit there wondering if my own travels down the Coast to Frisco and Mexico won't be just as sad and mad—but by bejesus j Christ

Excerpts from Jack Kerouac, *Desolation Angels*. Copyright © 1995 by Penguin Group USA.

it'll be bettern hangin around this rock. (Kerouac, *Desolation Angels*, 32)

After sixty days of solitude, Kerouac decides that he has done enough meditation and is starved for human affection. He remembers and describes his youth in Lowell as "tender, loving, and sad"; the word sadness permeates the book. He says, "O Ignorant brothers, O Ignorant sisters, O Ignorant me! There's nothing to write about, everything is nothing, there's everything to write about! — Time! Time! Things!" (Kerouac, *Desolation Angels*, 51). Again, we see a complex duality about his ideas concerning life and existence.

Kerouac writes in the beginning of the second section of the book titled "Desolation in the World":

... my friends ... were involved in the strictures of time and life, rather than the eternity and solitude of mountain snowy rocks ... and that everybody was goofing—wasting time—not being serious—trivial-in rivalries—timid before God—even the angels fighting ... (Kerouac, *Desolation Angels*, 66)

Kerouac is now extremely critical of society and the world and believes that many people lack spiritual awareness. He asks, "How can the universe be anything but a Womb?" Again, his worldview, beliefs, and theories on existence are becoming more complex and more fully developed, although a bit more cynical. Kerouac later writes:

The rivers of America and all the trees and all the green worlds in all those leaves and all the chlorotic molecules in all those green worlds and all the atoms in all those molecules, and all the infinite universes within all those atoms, and all our hearts and all our tissue and all our thoughts and all our brain cells and all the molecules and atoms in every cell, and all the infinite universes in every thought. ... (Kerouac, *Desolation Angels*, 88)

In this excerpt, Kerouac still has a worldview where he believes every infinitesimal physical element plays an important role, and we can see his reverence, admiration, and sense of awe in recognizing the details of the particularly unnoticed concepts that make life possible.

Kerouac also writes, "That which passes through everything has passed through me and always through my pencil and there is nothing to say" (Kerouac, *Desolation Angels*, 64). Here again, like in *The Scripture of the*

Golden Eternity and *Mexico City Blues*, we see oscillations and contradictions in that Kerouac believes that there is "nothing to say" but he feels compelled to write down his ideas. Equally important is that he has now come to affirm this sense of oneness with his writing and with the universe.

After Kerouac came down from Desolation Peak having already written half of what would be the published version of *Desolation Angels*, Viking Press informed him that his revised manuscript of *On the Road* was going to be released. Malcolm Cowley, the General Editor there, had been impressed with Kerouac's manuscript since 1951, but he believed that readers were not ready for the publication of a novel written in such a frenzied style. But by 1956, Cowley was making great efforts to get the novel published. Finally, on September 5, 1957, *On the Road* was published and was hailed by the reviewer Gilbert Millstein in *The New York Times*:

> *On the Road* is the second novel by Jack Kerouac, and its publication is a historic occasion insofar as the exposure of an authentic work of art is of any great moment in any age in which the attention is fragmented and the sensibilities are blunted by the superlatives of fashion. ...
>
> [The novel is] the most beautifully executed, the clearest and most important utterance yet made by the generation Kerouac himself named years ago as "beat" and whose principal avatar he is.
>
> Just as, more than any other novel of the Twenties, *The Sun Also Rises* came to be regarded as the testament of the Lost Generation, so it seems certain that *On the Road* will come to be known as that of the Beat Generation. (Charters, *On the Road*, III)

Kerouac and Joyce Johnson, a young writer he was living with, took their copy of *The New York Times*, and after Kerouac read this glowing review, he just shook his head "as if he couldn't figure out why he wasn't happier than he was" (Charters, *On the Road*, VIII). Joyce Johnson added, "Jack lay down obscure for the last time in his life. The ringing phone woke him the next morning and he was famous" (Charters, *On the Road*, VIII).

Three days later, the Sunday *Times* carried a review of the novel by David Dempsey titled, "In Pursuit of Kicks," which criticized Kerouac's subject matter and stated that Kerouac's road led *nowhere*. He also stated that the people Kerouac wrote about were a "sideshow of freaks"; *Time* magazine "compared Kerouac's writing to his recent attempts at painting with a mixture of house paint and glue" (Nicosia, 556). Unfortunately, the release of these critical assessments also "marked a turning point of public opinion against Kerouac that was never reversed in his lifetime" (Nicosia, 556).

The negative critical assessments only escalated, with *The Atlantic* finding the novel "monotonously repetitious," while the *Chicago Tribune* thought it "the completely uncontrolled product of an author who slobbers words" (Nicosia, 556). Yet, surprisingly, in the midst of all this criticism, Kerouac had become a center of attention at a national level and soon, Warner Brothers wanted to buy the movie rights for *On the Road*, offering him $150,000.

Reporters flocked to ask him questions about what the word "Beat" meant and after whom the real life characters of his novel were modeled. Regrettably, whenever Kerouac tried talking about other topics outside the lifestyle that his characters in his novel led, the reporters lost interest. "The reporters didn't care who *he* was, or how long he'd been working on his book, or what he was trying to do as a writer" (Charters, *On the Road*, IX).

When Kerouac told reporters that the word "Beat" was a word used to describe a state of "exalted exhaustion" or someone who is "sympathetic", but which was also somehow linked in "his mind to a Catholic beatific vision, the direct knowledge of God enjoyed by the blessed in heaven," they immediately lost interest (Charters, *On the Road*, IX). Kerouac soon became depressed because "this line of thought was obscure to most interviewers, who wanted a glib quote rather than a religious derivation of a hip slang term" (Charters, *On the Road*, IX). Sadly, this is the way Kerouac's public life continued.

Kerouac had begun drinking alcohol and whisky regularly years before the publication of *On the Road*, but not nearly as heavily as in the months following the release and public success and critical savaging of his book. His friends reminded him that fame was what he wanted throughout all these years, and now that he had it, he was not able to handle it. A fellow poet and friend of Kerouac, Gregory Corso, saw Kerouac a few months after the release of *On the Road*, and said he thought Kerouac was "a changed man"; what struck Corso

> ... most forcibly was finding Jack in the bathroom of a bar, sitting on a closed toilet seat, absolutely taken with himself, grooving in some private seventh heaven—for the first time in his life seemingly happy. Gregory figured, 'That's what he wanted, the man wanted acceptance.' Of course, he realized that Jack's drinking resulted in part from his deep feeling for the tragedy in life and from his being 'full of shadows at night.' (Nicosia, 577)

Kerouac began speaking angrily against fame, and as a means of "self-preservation he turned down offers to read all over the country, knowing that his stage fright always led to worse drinking" (Nicosia, 577). On the several television shows where he did appear, he was either harshly criticized, or he was too drunk to patiently and honestly answer any of the questions. For example, on John Wingate's *Night Beat* television interview, forty million people heard Kerouac say, "he was waiting for God to show his face" (Nicosia, 560).

The financial rewards of his book sales affected him as much as the fame. *On the Road* made the bottom of the bestseller list for several weeks, but then sales "faltered because Viking wasn't prepared to resupply the book stores rapidly enough" (Nicosia, 558). Because of its success, Viking Press decided to publish "an unabridged hardcover edition of *The Subterraneans*" (Nicosia, 559). This period also began the printing of other of Kerouac's books, many of which had been written many years before *On the Road*. Publically, Kerouac was still correcting the misconceptions about the Beat Generation. According to Allen Ginsberg, "there was a nationwide misperception that 'beat' meant 'angry at the world' rather than 'weeping at the world'" (Nicosia, 559). Nobody seemed to listen to what Kerouac was really saying. He tried to explain to his audiences and critics that *On the Road* had been written more than seven years before and that the characters in the novel were genuinely on a spiritual quest. He said in *Time* magazine on February 24, 1958, that

> The hero of *On the Road* is now a normal settled-down adult. He's a railroad conductor with three kids. I've seen him put the kids to bed, kneel down and say the Lord's prayer, and then maybe he'll sit down and watch television. (*Time*, 104)

Unfortunately, the explanations Kerouac gave were carelessly dismissed, and other explanations given by credible and notable critics like John Ciardi were taken more seriously. An article Ciardi wrote in *The Saturday Review* on July 12, 1959 harshly criticizes Kerouac's art:

> Fiction has been made of slighter materials than these when a writer has gone to work on it, but Kerouac has no interest in writing, if by writing one means the art of shaping experience into a form that releases the experience to a reader.
> Kerouac prefers merely to assert. There is nothing in this book (*Maggie Cassady*) that might reasonably be called a scene:

scenes must be paced and structured, and pace and structure are not available to the slap-sprawl school. There is no action here. Kerouac would have done well to remember Hemingway's warning to Marlene Dietrich, 'never [to] confuse motion with action.' Here, as everywhere in Kerouac's writing, there is more jerky motion and less action than one may find in any twentieth-century book I know of. There is not even anything that might pass as characterization, and perish the thought that there should be any development of character ... it is mistaken seriousness to treat this stuff as if it could be asked to respond to the criteria of serious writing. There is no interest here in the art of writing ... Kerouac obviously feels absolved from any necessity to make his material meaningful to the reader. Or even, for that matter, to show a trace of respect for the language itself. (Ciardi, *Saturday Review*, 22, 23)

John Ciardi excoriates Kerouac's art and, unfortunately, what critics like himself said always seemed to more consequential than anything that Kerouac himself said about his works. Comments and reviews like these haunted Kerouac and his writing until his death, and no matter what he said or what others said to defend his works, Kerouac would never be able to erase or replace the negative assessments that critics had of him and his writing. Only a few critics were supportive of Kerouac. For example, Henry Miller wrote at about the same time that Ciardi's piece was published:

When someone asks 'Where does Kerouac get that stuff?', say: 'From you!' He lay awake all night listening with eyes and ears. A night of a thousand years. Heard it in the womb, heard it in the cradle, heard it in school, heard it on the floor of life's stock exchange where dreams are traded for gold. (Miller)

Very few literary critics understood that Kerouac was trying to go beyond the confines and conventions of the traditional novel, hoping to merge the spirit, the heart, and writing with his spontaneous prose. He was seeking new territory and exploring new grounds, but with this kind of experimentation, he was either going to succeed greatly or disastrously fail.

Current critical assessments vary greatly on Kerouac, but if Kerouac's writing is both praised and criticized, so was his life's search. For with Kerouac the writing and the man doing the writing were one whole being. Those who look at his work carefully will see a devoted artist and individual focused on the single task of producing honest, spiritual writings, hoping to come to some kind of answer or truth that will make life's journey more bearable and more insightful for himself and his readers.

The second part of *Desolation Angels* presents a deeply spiritual, yet dejected individual whose writing allows him to tell his story from an extremely insightful and detailed point of view. He still often quotes Buddhist texts and makes references to Catholic beliefs. At one point he says, "Tao says, in more words than one, that a woman who takes care of her home has equalized Heaven and Earth" (Kerouac, *Desolation Angels*, 336). Here he is again referring to his mother; he speaks directly of her very tenderly in that same chapter:

> ... Here now I'm telling you about the most important person in this whole story and the best. I've noticed how most of my fellow writers all seem to 'hate' their mothers and make big Freudian or sociological philosophies around that, in fact using it as the straight theme of their fantasies, or at least saying as much—I often wonder if they've ever slept till four in the afternoon and woke up to see their mother darning their socks in a sad window light, or come back from revolutionary horrors of weekends to see her mending the rips in a bloody shirt with quiet eternal bowed head over needle—And not with martyred pose of resentment, either, but actually seriously bemused over mending, the mending of torture and folly and loss, mending the very days of your life with almost glad purposeful gravity—And when it's cold she puts on that shawl, and mends on, and on the stove potatoes are burbling forever—Making some neurotics go mad to see such sanity in a room—Making me mad sometimes because I'd been so foolish tearing shirts and losing shoes and losing and tearing hope to tatters in that silly thing called wild—'You've got to have an escape valve!' Julien'd often yelled at me, 'let out that steam or go mad!' tearing my shirt, only to have Memere two days later sitting in her chair mending that very shirt just because it was a shirt and it was mine, her son's—Not to make me feel guilty to hear her say: 'It was such a nice shirt, I paid $3.25 for it in Woolworth's, why do you let those nuts tear at your shirt like that? (Kerouac, *Desolation Angels*, 334)

Two chapters later, Kerouac mentions his father and writes: "I wonder what my father is saying in Heaven?" (337). Near the end of the book, Kerouac concludes that,

The only thing to do is be like my mother: patient, believing, careful, bleak, self-protective, glad for little flowers, suspicious of great
favors, beware of Greeks bearing Fish, make it your own way, hurt
no one, mind your own business, and make your compact with
God. For God is our Guardian Angel and this is a fact that's only
proven when proof exists no more.
    Eternity, and Here—and—Now, are the same thing.
Send that message back to Mao, or Schlesinger at Harvard, or
Herbert Hoover too. (Kerouac, *Desolation Angels*, 340)

Kerouac's worldview comes into clear focus and readers now see a very
spiritual, mature soul. He reaches conclusions after giving life careful thought
and examination. Because of these rambling, seemingly over-simplified
perspectives, critics dismissed Kerouac altogether and he, in turn, began to
dismiss the world.

Chapter 8

Jack Kerouac's Final Years

By the end of *Desolation Angels* Kerouac's spirit seems tired of his own restlessness and seems to recede into a despondent worldview. He writes:

> ... Later I'm back in New York sitting around with Irwin and Simon and Raphael and Lazarus, and now we're famous writers more or less, but they wonder why I'm so sunk now, so unexcited as we sit among all our published books and poems, tho at least, since I live with *Memere* in a house of her own miles from the city, it's a peaceful sorrow. A peaceful sorrow at home is the best I'll ever be able to offer the world, in the end, and so I told my Desolation Angels goodbye. A new life for me. (Kerouac, *Desolation Angels*, 366)

And Kerouac did just that. He began a new life that we can describe as reclusive. "The man he had been in 1950 who had written *On the Road* he was only second cousin to now, and yet people invariably looked at him, spoke to him, and deferred to him, as if he was that other man, for the Beat Generation was news by then, and Kerouac (they thought) *was* the Beat Generation" (Holmes, *Nothing More to Declare*, 591). As a result, Kerouac made his last road trip to seek his new life, accompanied now not by any of the other Beats, but by his mother, and they were in search not for kicks, but a house to live in—a house they could call a home.

Despite generally negative critical assessments, Kerouac was not wholly abandoned by critics and friends. Dan Wakefield very generously says of *Desolation Angels* in 1965,

> ... We do not yet know what literary fruits the new life has produced, but there is no doubt that this book is a fine ending for the old Life. If the Pulitzer Prize in fiction were given for the book that is most representative of American life, I would nominate *Desolation Angels*.

> Of course, the judges would probably cast it aside as some kind of
> dangerous, antisocial tract about the lives of a group of rebellious
> oddballs. We seldom recognize a real American Dream when we
> see one. (Wakefield, *Atlantic Monthly*, 72)

John Clellon Holmes, a great friend to Kerouac until the day of his death, has some very insightful and valuable comments about the writer and man he knew Kerouac to be. Holmes says that after he read the first 120-foot-long draft of *On the Road*,

> ... it disturbed me, for in it I caught my first glimpse of the Kerouac
> to come, a Kerouac for whom I was oddly unprepared: a lonely,
> self-communing, mind-stormed man still devout, though in a ruin
> of faiths; persistently celebrating whatever flower had managed to
> survive our bitter, urban weeds; indefatigable of eye, and funny of
> mind; haunted by a reflex of love in the very pit of rude sensation; and
> above all, hankering—hankering for an end: for truth to finally end
> the relativism, for harmony to somehow end the violence, so that
> peace would come to the young of this era, who were the heirs of
> both—and, failing that, for death. Something murmured behind the
> reckless onrush of the prose. It wasn't quite audible, but it accounted
> for the note of distant, fleeting sibilance that reverberated within the
> book's headlong syncopations. And for the first time, I suspected
> that underneath his youthful energy and jubilant thirst for life this
> man was immeasurably old in his soul.
> It is difficult to articulate, but as the years have passed he has
> seemed more and more an old spirit to me; folk-old, poet-old,
> not of this world; like a ragged, tipsy old Li Po, thrashing around
> down there in the river marshes, muttering verses to himself by
> his fire of twigs in the dusk, allowing reality to pass through him
> unobstructed, writing messages back from solitude. (Holmes,
> *Nothing More to Declare*, 587)

Kerouac was tired and worn out by 1957, and his worldview demanded a need for solitude, a need that the constant nagging of reporters and admirers did not allow. "Literary fame had the effect of breaking ties with nearly all he had known as security" and although few ties were left for Kerouac, "his resources for overcoming the new divisions were few, and little could come of it" (Dardess, 298).

Still, Kerouac kept writing, and he conceived yet another full-length novel three years later, *Big Sur*, along with collections of short pieces in his book

Lonesome Traveler. Big Sur "marks the end of the unhappy affair with fame. The media had grown tired of making fun of the Beats and their king, and Kerouac, now left alone, grew lonely" (Dardess, 300). Jack Kerouac moved back in with his mother and began revisiting his boyhood town of Lowell.

These visits were positive for Kerouac and "imposed a much needed shape on his life" (300).

However, his life was rapidly collapsing. In 1958, he received the first of several barroom beatings, and in 1960, at the age of 38, he suffered his first attack of "delirium tremens" (a severe form of alcohol withdrawal which involves sudden and severe mental or nervous system changes) (Dardess, 299). These problems would continue; Kerouac became a victim of himself: he could not handle fame, not even when his books were reviewed with high praise.

Throughout the 1960s, Kerouac wanted to standardize the names in all his published books in order to present "one multi-episode but connected account of one life and vision" (Dardess, 300). When his publishers ignored his requests in fear of libel, he began drinking even more heavily. Yet in the midst of all his drinking binges, Kerouac still found time to write. In 1965, he wrote *Satori in Paris*, an account of a trip he made alone to France to research his family tree. Kerouac's writing reflects a free spirit, as if he has,

> ... nothing to lose, least of all his dignity. He could parody himself; he could laugh without bitterness or guilt at his own follies and those of his readers. But from behind the laughter could echo the sound characteristic of all Kerouac's writing, the sound of his compassion for the endless suffering of all mortal beings. (Dardess, 301)

Kerouac always remained faithful to his writing and he "sought strenuously and successfully to realize that virtue in practice" (Dardess, 302). Because Kerouac's search is largely rooted deeply in spirituality, his honesty validates his search that much more for his readers:

> An assessment of Kerouac's literary accomplishments must be expressed in paradoxes if it is to avoid simplification. The spontaneous prose method itself is a paradoxical instrument: consciously formed yet unconsciously, intuitively practiced. It is a method designed for those who, like Kerouac himself, are already masters of the conventional modes of writing. It is a step beyond literary

formality, not an escape from it. It uses such formality as the basis upon which the inner mind can articulate its contrasting effects. ...

Kerouac's true position in American Literature will never become clear until he is measured against standards which he himself set and which were legitimized over a century earlier by no less an authority than Emerson. Kerouac is still held hostage, however, by the Cold War prejudices that originally condemned his work. It is perhaps a sadder thought that such prejudices can last so long that one writer has suffered from them. Kerouac's literary reputation has become a test of the American intellectual climate since World War II: a climate not much less gray and forbidding now than it was twenty-five years ago. (Dardess, 302)

Since the 1950s, Jack Kerouac has introduced many readers to the vision that he had as a writer, a vision of reporting the truth from within his soul. His unique vision of life validates personal achievement. As a writer, faithfulness to individual craft and design is essential. If we measure Kerouac by that standard, he triumphed. If we measure how dedicated he was to his craft, again he triumphs.

Jack Kerouac's search for an epiphany was an honest, complex, developmental, ongoing process. His honesty and effort to examine his own life is virtuous and admirable; we could maybe even say, too absolute. There is no doubt that Kerouac's vision of writing powerfully and emphatically influenced other members of the Beat Generation. Allen Ginsberg says that Kerouac taught him a great deal about writing poetry. William Burroughs equally praises Kerouac's daringness to experiment and develop his own writing skills with such dedication. And John Clellon Holmes says that Kerouac's writing is a living testament of the man himself.

More importantly, when evaluating Jack Kerouac's works we must ask ourselves the fundamental question, "What should literature do?" Literature should open our eyes to the broadness of the world and should make us question not only life in the general sense, but the purpose of our own individual lives. Literature should help bring life into focus. Literature should affect us in some significant way, and Jack Kerouac's literature has profoundly affected many readers. His life story is filled with fascinating discovery; his books explore the conditions of his soul and, in turn, allow us to reflect on the conditions of our own souls. What Kerouac concluded from all his searches and what his works attempt to express was, indeed, as John Clellon Holmes says, "A stubborn feeling for the heart that beats beneath our masquerades, which, as I've gotten older, seems to be the only part of wisdom on which I'll stand" (Holmes, *Gone in October*, 16).

In conclusion, let us turn to the words of Ralph Waldo Emerson from his essay "Nature" published in 1836:

> ... Wise men pierce this rotten diction and fasten words once again to visible things, so that the picturesque language is at once a commanding certificate that he who employs it is in allegiance with truth and God. ... The imagery is spontaneous. It is the blending of experience with the present action of the mind. (Rpt. in Dardess, 302)

Emerson's essay, "Intellect" states: "Our spontaneous action is always best ... Our thinking is a pious reception ..." (Dardess, 302). Kerouac, perhaps an equal to many of our greatest writers, successfully achieved this blending.

Kerouac's writing has enlarged the possibility of a "new American poetics" (Charters, XIV). His efforts have directly changed the possibilities of literature in America, and his experimentalism with writing style shows a dedicated, faithful artist at work. Kerouac's place in literature may yet be uncertain, but without doubt, his personal searches reveal a man who was faithfully living and following the callings of his life. And for this reason alone, if for no other, we should give credit to Jack Kerouac the man, if not Jack Kerouac the writer.

Works Cited

Allen, Donald, ed. *Jack Kerouac: Good Blonde and Others*. San Francisco: Grey Fox Press, 1993.

Baym, Nina, et al, eds. *The Norton Anthology of American Literature*. 4th ed., vol. 2. New York: W. W. Norton and Company, 1994.

Charters, Ann, ed. *The Portable Beat Reader*. New York: Penguin Books, 1992.

Charters, Ann and John Dardess, eds. *The Beats: Literary Bohemians in Postwar America; Part (A—L) and Part 2 (M—Z). Dictionary of Literary Biography: Volume 16*. Detroit: Gale Research Company, 1983. Detroit: Gale Research Company, 1983.

Clark, Tom. *Jack Kerouac*. New York: Harcourt Brace Jovanovich, 1984.

Donaldson, Scott, ed. *Jack Kerouac, On The Road: Text and Criticism*. New York: Penguin Books, 1979.

Ginsberg, Allen. *Howl and Other Poems*. San Francisco: City Lights Books, 1956.

Holmes, John Clellon. *Gone In October: Last Reflections on Jack Kerouac*. Hailey, ID: The Limberlost Press, 1985.

Holmes, John Clellon. *Nothing More To Declare*. New York: E.P. Dutton and Company, 1967.

Huebel, Harry Russell. *Jack Kerouac. Boise State University Western Writers Series*, Number 39. Boise, ID: The Caxton Printers Ltd., 1979.

Kerouac, Jack. *The Town and the City*. New York: Harcourt Brace Jovanovich, Publishers, 1983.

Kerouac, Jack. *On The Road*. New York: Penguin Books, 1991.

Kerouac, Jack. *The Dharma Bums*. New York: Penguin Books, 1986.

Kerouac, Jack. *The Subterraneans*. New York: Grove Weidenfeld, 1981.

Kerouac, Jack. *Mexico City Blues*. New York: Grove Weidenfeld, 1990.

Kerouac, Jack. *Visions of Cody*. New York: Penguin Books, 1993.

Kerouac, Jack. *The Scripture of the Golden Eternity*. New York: Corinth Books, 1970.

Kerouac, Jack. *Tristessa*. New York: Penguin Books, 1992.

Kerouac, Jack. *Book of Dreams*. San Francisco: City Lights Books, 1981.

Kerouac, Jack. *Visions of Gerard*. New York: Penguin Books, 1991.

Kerouac, Jack. *Desolation Angels*. New York: Wideview and Pedigree, 1980.

Kerouac, Jack. *Satori in Paris*. New York: Grove Press, 1966.

Knight, Arthur and Kit Knight, eds. *Jack Kerouac: Dear Carolyn, Letters to Carolyn Cassady*. California, PA: Aspect Composition, 1983.

McNally, Dennis. *Desolate Angel: Jack Kerouac, the Beat Generation, and America*. New York: Random House, 1979.

Mack, Maynard, et al. *The Norton Anthology of World Masterpieces*, 5th ed., vol. 2. New York: W.W. Norton and Company, 1985.

Nicosia, Gerald. *Memory Babe: A Critical Biography of Jack Kerouac*. New York: Grove Press, 1983.

Portuges, Paul. *The Visionary Poetics of Allen Ginsberg*. Santa Barbara, CA: Ross-EriksonPublishers, 1978.

Ross, Nancy Wilson. *Three Ways of Asian Wisdom: Hinduism, Buddhism, Zen, and Their Significance for the West*. New York: Simon and Schuster, 1966.

Smith, Paul. *The Humanities: Cultural Roots and Continuities: Volume II—The Humanities and the Modern World*, 3rd ed. Lexington, KY: D.C. Heath and Company, 1989.

Tytell, John. *Naked Angels: The Lives and Literature of the Beat Generation*. New York: McGraw-Hill, 1976.

Wakefield, Dan. "Jack Kerouac Comes Home." *The Atlantic*, July, 1965.

CPSIA information can be obtained
at www.ICGtesting.com
Printed in the USA
LVHW080026221218
601391LV00012B/69/P